UPON A MIDNIGHT CLEAR

T0278864

More Christmas Epiphanies

Upon a Midnight Clear

EDITED BY JJ LEE

Published by Tidewater Press
New Westminster, BC, Canada
tidewaterpress.ca

978-1-990160-44-8 (print)
978-1-990160-45-5 (e-book)

An early version of"Songbird" by Jill Maynard first published in *emerge 21*
An early version of "Our Book of Days" by Jane Harris first published as "What I Learned from the Deer—a Conversation with My Dead Son" in *yolkLiterary Digital Edition,* January 4, 2024

LIBRARY AND ARCHIVES CANADA CATALOGUING IN PUBLICATION
Title: Upon a midnight clear : more Christmas epiphanies / edited by JJ Lee.
Other titles: Upon a midnight clear (Compilation)
Names: Lee, J. J. (James-Jason), editor.
Identifiers: Canadiana (print) 2024047936X | Canadiana (ebook) 20240486366 | ISBN 9781990160448 (softcover) | ISBN 9781990160455 (EPUB)
Subjects: LCSH: Christmas—Canada—Anecdotes. | LCGFT: Anecdotes.
Classification: LCC GT4987.15 .U66 2024 | DDC 394.26630971—dc23

TIDEWATER
PRESS

Contents

To Melissa, Emmet, and Jack, who make all seasons merry and bright.

INTRODUCTION

JJ LEE

The human heart travels quite far in *Upon a Midnight Clear*.

From Spain to Maui, Tunisia to Ireland, Texas to north of the Canadian treeline, this second collection of true-life, worst-case-scenario Christmases finds our storytellers going great distances to confront feelings of alienation, abandonment, and loss during what is supposed to be the merriest month on the calendar. Despite the long, diverging journeys that trace all over the map, everyone seems to follow the same bright star in the sky, the star of hope.

I too point to that light when asked why I would wish to collect such a woeful, often funny, roster of tales. In each, courage, persistence, and a certain wilful blindness are summoned in the face of truly trying circumstances. You could say that we find people here at their best in the worst of times and at their worst in the best of times. But as they follow the long road, all strive to attain, hold, and offer the peace and love we associate with the season.

I hope you find their hard-earned epiphanies as overwhelming and humbling as I do.

P.S. Thank you to Kilmeny Jane Denny and Lynn Duncan for giving life to and sustaining this growing series. Here's to another one.

The Gift

MICHAEL MCLEAN

I put myself through school while working full-time as a security guard. I attended classes by day and did an eight-hour shift until midnight at the mall.

I would ditch the university with Burnaby in my rearview and Surrey in my sights. My ride was a gold 1980 Mazda 626. Not a spring chicken, but she held her own. No rust, no dents, engine purring like a kitten. She was my sanctuary for the forty-minute haul to the job. The speakers, a recent splurge, blasted my tunes, drowning out the world.

The Guildford mall was a behemoth that sprawled over five hundred hectares, a monolith of grey concrete and brick. It had windows clouded with urban grime that, all through the early part of the fall semester, mirrored the harsh afternoon sun. The south entrance connected to the main artery and had the most foot traffic. Inside, the air was a cocktail of fast food and stale smoke; the ghosts of a thousand stories lingering in the sealed HVAC air.

The mall was so big it sprawled north across the street, joined by an overpass, to a quieter section. There was an inconspicuous door, tucked like a secret, that opened to a stairwell that led to a janitor's closet that had been converted to a security hub. It had the smell of a gym locker on a bad day. The guards used it as a refuge from the mall's crowds. The hub had a changing room, lunchroom, coffee break room, and a haven for tall tales, all crammed into a windowless, forty square feet under the stairs.

On the job as security, I wasn't a patient person.

I often did not get a great night's sleep. I had submitted myself to a demanding schedule. I thought, back then, I had something to prove not only to myself but to all those who claimed I was not smart enough or good enough. I was a survivor. I told my brothers time and again, "That we lived through that shit and came out the other side without criminal records, and sane enough to participate in society, is a badge of honour."

I had trouble accepting simple kindnesses. If someone at school said, "I believe in you," I thought that person was phony, and the act was simply performed out of politeness.

I was proud, angry, and alone. I cared for myself. In Jane Eyre, Charlotte Bronte wrote, "The more solitary, the more friendless, the more unsustained I am, the more I will respect myself." That was me. No one was going to hold me back from achieving and gaining a real sense of accomplishment, except me. All this would manifest in frustration, not only with myself but with others.

A mall customer or shop owner would be explaining an incident and go into excruciating detail. Silently I would be saying, "Just get to the point." I'm sure the occasional eyeroll occurred. As I took notes, I would do the hand-roll gesture as a way of demonstrating my impatience. I should add that, to the people I knew, I would also be very direct. I'd pretend to fall asleep or interject saying, "It all started when I was six," or "Jesus wrote a shorter book, bro, cut to the chase."

My tank was running on empty, and I was throwing myself the best pity party you ever saw. That's what I was feeling when the semester ended and I agreed to work the Christmas week.

Everywhere I looked, there was a seasonal reminder of my inadequacy. I think everyone hopes "this Christmas will be better than the last one" and yet I always failed to prepare for it. Like it is supposed to happen spontaneously. Christmas was more or less just another day to me, or so I tried to convince myself.

Growing up, Christmas was always a tough time. My mother could barely afford to keep a roof over our heads, let alone buy presents for seven children. A reality I only understood later, when it was far too late to say it's okay. I was never the person who would hand-craft a snowglobe out of a mason jar, acorns, and unicorn tears. I saved money and did not buy gifts for people other than Christmas cards. When I received them, I tossed them in the trash soon after Christmas was over.

So, at the mall, I was apathetic toward Christmas. There

were stores decorated with plastic trees and wreaths; the scent of cinnamon was everywhere. There was a booth where people paid to have their gifts professionally wrapped. I saw these as pretentious trappings and fake paraphernalia. I took a long look around that shopping mall at the people with their packages. I got angry, almost enough to save myself from the feeling of envy. I needed that little bit of righteous anger. I remember even muttering to myself how I hated this time of year.

Staring at Santa's Castle didn't help. It was on a lower level at the centre of the mall where all four halls converged, a peaked house with windows on all four walls. There were Styrofoam candy canes and the usual decor over the red exterior. It was surrounded by reindeer statues in cotton snow. I found myself peering over the edge from the upper level watching people and their children milling in and out of it. "Here Comes Santa Claus" was playing over the music system because he was due to sit on his throne.

This Santa had a real beard and looked surprisingly like the advertisement on the Coke commercials. He was also just as jolly and friendly. He played the part well and people scrambled to take a picture with him. I thought they were entitled and pretentious; their children spoiled, overly privileged brats, ignorant of what it was like to make something out of nothing.

That somehow made me feel superior to them because

they would never know what I knew. When I was a child, I thought of Santa Claus as a saviour who rescued children. Now he was just a portly man in a red suit paid to act the part created by an advertising agency. I stood amongst these people, my bad attitude firmly intact.

When I put on that security uniform, it somehow emboldened me. I engaged in conversation with strangers: men, women, teenagers, families. When I spoke to them, there was no expectation. I never knew how they were going to respond—or even if they were going to respond—but they always felt compelled to reply because I was an employee of the mall. I would notice a certain shop that they just visited, then say something like, "I love that store, bought my last pair of shoes there, super comfortable." Sometimes that would lead to more conversation, sometimes not. I really had no ulterior motive, other than to either confirm or change my first impression. I met all the women that I dated this way but, like I said, this was never my intention.

I struck up a conversation with an older woman going to sit on the bench against the glass railing. She had several bags and when she put them down one of them tipped over. A can of spray snow rolled out and tapped my shoe. I reached down to pick it up and hand it to her. I said I remembered the days of real snow in Dawson Creek, where the drifts were sometimes higher than the door of your house.

She said she was a former farm girl and recalled similar days of real snow, that she'd come to the Lower Mainland to retire. I think that's when I went into my rant about what Christmas was like when I was a kid. Filled with play and not presents. I said, "Christmas was taking my toboggan out to my favourite hill at the back of the Royal Canadian Legion in the small village of Pouce Coupe, BC where we would slide until it was dark. The bonfire we built at the bottom made the slide even better. I would stay there until my jeans froze over top of my long underwear. We'd take turns pulling each other home, lying back on the toboggan staring at the star-filled skies through the zipped-up hoods of our jackets, looking for Santa Claus."

The woman got up and said "that sounds about right" in a futile attempt to placate me before she walked away. I leaned over the railing again, looking down at the castle. An old man next to me said, "You're from DC area?"

I said, "Oh, yes. Spent many years in Dawson Creek before our family moved to Pouce Coupe."

He shook his head. "I used to live in Dawson Creek as well."

His brown hair was short and parted on the side, which suited his round hairless white face. He was slightly overweight but not overly so, a dad-bod some people would call it nowadays. He wore a grey, waist-length Columbia jacket with a blue-collared shirt under it, blue jeans, and brown

Docker shoes. He wore a little too much aftershave and was shorter than I was. Most people are. Back then I stood six feet five inches and weighed 190 pounds. His smile was open and friendly, and he had a good solid handshake. The kind of handshake where you knew it was a practised gesture.

I replied, "Really? Whereabouts did you live?"

He said that it was a hole in the wall on top of the hill.

I said, "Oh boy, yes, I am familiar with those places. We used to live there as well."

Then he looked leaned in even closer, studying me. And I studied him.

He raised his arm slightly, finger pointing at my chest. "Do you know a woman named Mary?"

"Mary? That's my mother's name."

Mary rarely said, "I love you."

She was a tough woman who was silent most of the time. The exception was when she was telling you to do something or yelling at you for perceived wrongdoing. In those circumstances, she would mix English with Cree, her first language. She always finished with " . . . just you never mind!"

If I persisted in wrongdoing, the next step for her was the belt, strap, spoon, extension cord, broom—whatever she could grab to hit me with.

*

She was not very motherly. We cooked for ourselves most of the time with whatever was in the cupboards or refrigerator, which was never much. My mother was prone to wandering off for days, even weeks at a time. She did have the common sense never to drink at home for fear "the welfare" would take us again.

The first time that happened we were still living in Edmonton. My aunts were caring for us at the time, but they were in their early twenties. They had a large and loud party the previous night with people coming into and out of the house, smashing bottles and spinning tires out front. My siblings and I cowered in one room the whole night, hearing the loud voices, the arguing, the fistfights on the lawn. Sometimes people would open the bedroom door, looking for a private place. We huddled together, trying to make our infant brother stop crying from hunger.

The next morning, we woke up to silence and walked downstairs to see the house trashed with bottles and glass everywhere. Crushed cigarettes on the carpet and the smell of beer in the air. The curtains were closed, which made the living room dark, but the sun still peeked through in the dining room and kitchen.

My older brother, who was nine, casually went to the stove and started boiling a pot of water for porridge. My aunts got up and tripped over a couple of men asleep on the floor in the living room. They heard a car pull up in front of the house and cracked the curtains to see a four-door red car with the ministry logo on the door. They scrambled around the house waking up the sleeping men, who ran out the back just as we heard three knocks at the door.

Before I could understand the situation, I was stepping from that red car into the cool autumn morning and gazing at an orphanage draped in its cold white concrete, not unlike the Guildford mall. The many windows with bars seemed to glare down at me like I wasn't invited, but the large metal door swung open all too easily. I walked inside, then stopped and shuffled at the entrance in the shoes I shared with my brother. We were barely a year apart in age and so we shared everything. He had nothing else to wear so he was in his bare feet.

I smelled medicine and cleaning fluid. A nun came towards us. She had on a long grey dress and black bib that covered her large head and framed her stern face. "Six more you bring?" she asked in a French accent.

The man in the trench coat and glasses read from a note-book. "Yes, Native Indian, ages infant to nine years old."

"And how old are you, young man?" She leaned over me, smiling. It was a smile I had come to expect from white faces. The judgement in that smile was as thick as a piece of bannock and just as salty.

I furrowed my brows and looked down at my feet. I held up five fingers.

*

"Okay then, follow me," she instructed.

All of us were separated by age and gender. My younger brother did not have dark skin like I did. He had dirty blond hair. He was marched off to be with the white children in the orphanage. Suddenly I was alone, but I was calm.

As a child (and even now as an adult) I was very aware of all the parts of reality that were better. Like a kid with an ice cream cone, or a family in the park, or a kid on a bike. I wished it was me. So when I was being told to leave a store when others were allowed in, or being searched as I left a store while others walked by and stared, I could always recall what was normal and compare it to what we were as a family, and to myself as an individual.

I noticed people who didn't get thrown out of stores: how they acted, how they dressed. The analysis, in my young mind, came through a self-aware lens of shame, humility, and inadequacy, because I was not that. I was embarrassed to be me.

But when I was with my family, I wasn't the only one suffering that way. Up until that moment, my brothers, sisters and I were inseparable. We fought and argued, to be sure, but we were never lonely so long as we had each other. They were more than just siblings, they were my friends, best friends.

But here we were, separated. I had no idea it was for adoption purposes. All I knew was that I was by myself, and

I felt dead inside. Nothing had any meaning anymore. I had no idea where our mother was, and perhaps I didn't care. I do not recall experiencing any sense of desperation; I do recall having night terrors and sleepwalking. Perhaps that was a result of my denial.

One afternoon, slipping into a locked area to visit my infant brother in a crib, I noticed that he wasn't crying. Why wasn't he crying?

The months carried on. Very slowly, I adjusted to this new reality. I noticed decorations began to appear around the building. No one ever spoke of it but I knew what was going on. Before we were taken, I had learned about Santa Claus by watching CBC television. Children received presents from him so long as you wrote him a letter. I asked my sister to help me write but there was no paper and nothing to write with. It seems silly looking back, but I got my sister to scratch our address with a fork on a piece of wood trim I found in a cupboard and threw it out the door into the snow. If Santa was magic, he would find it, but I feared Santa would not know where I was. Could he even come here?

In the orphanage there were many pieces of religious iconography around: crosses, pictures of Jesus on the walls, and Bibles. There were also decorations like wreaths, a tree, and some garland around the office area but not in the hallways. Would Santa visit this sterile and spartan place? I guess I did hold a sliver of hope, but it was fading with each passing day. No one spoke of Christmas and, after that first day, the nuns never spoke to me at all.

The days in that place seemed to blend together into one long day. I was waiting for something to happen, anything. I felt powerless and got lost inside my head wondering what was coming next. I felt like a caged animal that once had endless prairie to explore. I had a depression like none other, a boredom that rivalled the longest rainy day. I would sit on the edge of the bed, head hung low, sometimes crying, staring at my feet. I would wish that Santa Claus, if he was magical, would come and get me. It was the single hope that I hung onto.

Then the long day ended. The nun dressed in grey arrived at the doorway of the ward. She said, "Put your shoes on, you have to go now."

I froze in fear, my hands playing with fingers at my chest. My lips quivered. "Where?"

The nun grabbed my hair and pulled me toward the door. She pushed me down the hall, the sound of her shoes echoing behind me. I stumbled. Where was I going? The big metal door opened, and I was pushed through, with no fanfare or words spoken. It slammed behind me.

My eyes widened to see my brothers and sisters running toward my mom, who stood by a car parked in front. I was delighted to see her but at the same time ambivalent. I actually recall running part way, then walking the rest. My feet were frozen by the time I got in the car. Once more, I piled into a car, my face pressed firmly against the window, going to another unknown place. That'd be Dawson Creek.

I should say we ended up there because the money and the gas ran out. And we stayed.

It became home for the remainder of my formative years. It was a place where the haves and the have-nots mixed uncomfortably, and again, judgement was everywhere. It was a place where white privilege was business as usual.

We moved into one of the single-room duplexes built by American soldiers when they constructed the Alaska Highway. They were remnants left over from a different era with no heater, just a pot-belly stove in the corner, and no insulation. There were no beds, no couches, no furniture of any kind. My mother had left everything meaningful behind in Edmonton. She was never burdened by such nostalgic things. We eventually did get a kitchen table but only three chairs. I had to stand at the table to eat.

That season, I felt that special kind of cold you find in northern British Columbia, where your breath will freeze in the open air and ice will form an inch thick on a plastic-wrapped window. I met our poverty with my strange form of silent acceptance. I spent hours poring over a torn and dog-eared Sears catalogue, one of my few means of entertainment. The cover said it all: *The Christmas Wish Book.*

Still unable to write a letter, I asked my mom instead to show Santa the pictures of the presents I wanted him to bring me.

"Get that away!" my mom yelled.

She swiped the book to the floor. I dove for it and picked it up in a protective way, staring back at her, expecting the stick. I uncreased the battered, still precious, pages. They were more than just pictures in a book to me. I never showed her the catalogue again.

Christmas Eve came and there was no tree. The house was void of seasonal trappings. There were no signs of Christmas here at all. Then came three knocks on the door, just like the knocks I heard when we were taken.

Why was it always three knocks?

My head snapped toward the door, and I felt the electricity of that last rap.

My mom opened it slowly. There stood a man with a freshly cut pine tree.

"Ho, Ho, Ho," he said. The paper-thin walls of the duplex we lived in had let our neighbour in on the sounds of our near-relentless sobbing. But he had also heard all our hopes and dreams.

I could smell the pine from across the room as he brought the tree through the door. I spent the rest of the day helping set that tree up. The Christmas decorations consisted of popcorn on thread, egg-carton creations, and newspaper snowflakes. It wasn't much to look at really, but it was ours and I was proud of the hours we spent.

There was one small string of lights strategically placed so that it lit up the room. I slept under that tree staring at them all night, getting lost in dreams.

When I woke a few hours later, in the early morning, there was an absence of presents under the tree. I tried not to cry. It didn't work. I sat cross-legged in the corner with my head in my hands, tears streaming, staring at my dirt-stained feet, the weight of everything slowly crushing me. But I made no sound. Mom always said, "Stop crying or I'll give you something to cry about."

Then another three taps. I held my breath. Again, Mom answered the door again. The man held black garbage bags brimming with carefully wrapped items.

He said, "I think Santa delivered these to the wrong house." Those paper-thin walls had inspired this man to spend what little money he had on six almost-orphans so they could have a Christmas to remember, my first Christmas.

The toys were previously loved items. The broken pieces and missing wheels didn't matter. I got to open something. There was a set of Matchbox cars and six pieces of orange racing track. There was a cowboy holster and six-guns. I couldn't think of a time I'd ever been happier. In fact, until that moment, there were only two things in the world that made me happy: ice cream and the Montreal Canadiens. I knew every player and watched most games when a television was available.

I opened my final gift and grinned from ear to ear. A pair of skates.

I didn't know how to skate, but I was elated to have a pair of my own. With those skates, I could learn to fly like my hero Savard or tend goal like Dryden. The leather was a bit scarred, but the blades were sharp. There were letters stencilled on the inside "N-E-I-L". It spelled a word I had never heard before. I asked the man what it meant.

He said, "These are genuine Neil skates. No one else in the world has these skates. These are very special."

That evening, there was no Christmas dinner, no dinner at all, just some saltines with cheese and a glass of milk. Again, I slept on the wooden floor under the tree, skates in hand, using my jacket for a pillow.

That first winter in Dawson Creek, they were far too big for me. To fit into them, I stuffed wool socks in the front. I never learned to float on the ice like Savard, but I did learn to skate. For many years, I used those skates, and my understanding of the significance of that day increased as I grew older. I cherished them.

Many Christmases would pass in Dawson Creek and later in Pouce Coupe.

There were torturous events. I have memories of my siblings and me comparing battle scars in our rooms. We would ask each other, "What did you do?" And the answer would be, "There was no more cold tea" or "I left a spoon in the sink."

When those disclosures were over, then came the revealing of the welts that an extension cord could make on a child's back. There were empty bowls and hardships. I watched two white boys beat up a kid near the entrance of the high school. They washed that kid's face with new-fallen snow and said, "There, now you're white!"

The words echoed and bounced around in my head. Fear froze me in place. I pulled my jacket down to hide my brown skin. Other kids walked past the boy lying on the ground, covered in snow.

"Don't look at him," I thought to myself.

This was when I knew I was a First Nations person capable of denying my proud heritage in order to survive. There was shame in that thought, soul-crushing shame that I did not help my brother off the ground.

Can I say, despite all that I'm telling you here, it wasn't all bad? That it seems that way because maybe the bad is what I remember the most? At the time, I had a coping skill. l pictured bad moments on a giant blackboard and erased them with broad strokes of a brush.

They say that a bad parent was once a traumatized child, caught in their own chaotic intensity and suffering. The poetry of their soul is lost in so many crosswinds. I believe that to be true. But I would sense a bigger picture. There is an untravelled, tumultuous sea to forgiveness and perhaps the challenge was to somehow keep your spirit intact while you found a way to sail across it.

My self-awareness caught a glimpse of the blackboard and told me that this was not how it should be. Somewhere along the journey, I would find my path, learn to heal, learn to love, and be the person I would approve of. Maybe I could become the antithesis of the way I was raised and start a new circle, one that could spring new growth in the rotted remnants of a childhood. I made myself one promise: to never be hungry again.

These ideas grew firm and stayed with me. They made me work hard to get far from the limited existence I was guaranteed in northern British Columbia. With $300 in my jeans and a heart filled with courage, I was determined to start anew in Vancouver. When I first arrived, I was met by the same old familiar starvation. I even ate crab-apples from trees to feed myself. I held on for better days and I never let one Christmas pass without telling someone—a neighbour, a new friend, a girlfriend—about the man next door. I would show them my skates.

The old man in the mall dropped his hands to his side. He took one step closer. He said "Do you remember one Christmas . . ."

His voice cracked and I didn't let him finish.

"You . . . it was you." I pointed back at him. "You were the man next door."

He nodded, his eyes glazed.

I told him, "I tell the story of that Christmas every year to whoever will listen to it." I continued, "What you did, it changed my life."

I stood there in disbelief. Twenty years and many miles separated then and now. Yet in this small corner of the world, in a mall in Surrey, there we were. I wondered, "Why here and why now?"

He told me that back in those days he had been working on the oil rigs and had been laid off. Those days of no work turned into weeks and, soon enough, he had fallen into poverty he thought would never end. He said, "I knew Dawson Creek wasn't the place for me if I wanted to change."

He said that, after that Christmas day, opportunity opened the door for him to transform. He didn't say how. We just veered into some small talk about the who, what, and wheres. When we were done, I said, "You know, all these years I never knew your name."

"Neil," he said, holding out his hand. "It's a pleasure to meet you again."

I must have been stunned because, when he invited me to his home for a Christmas dinner, I actually accepted.

Socializing was uncomfortable for me. I had to excuse

myself. I left that centre court and focused on my job. I can't tell you the steps, the ways or the means, of the rest of that shift. I was lost in the magnitude of the moment. I was floating, trapped in a daydream, asking myself, "How could this be?"

Everything that happened to me, from that childhood Christmas morning to meeting him now, all the things in between. I felt the eradication of doubt, fear, and anxiety. It was being replaced by confidence, courage, and purpose. It was as real as the security keys I held in my hand. Afterward, I took step by ever-astonished step.

It still seems supernatural. The strong winds of revelation still scatter my thoughts in every direction.

The next evening I had Christmas Eve dinner with a family I had never met.

I stepped out of my car and into the drizzle. The rain fell like a soft whisper as I opened my umbrella. I hesitated for a moment before knocking three times. I almost shut my eyes. I was anxious and my thoughts raced.

Neil's son answered the door. Neil introduced me and led me around the corner into his palatial home. The stairs spiralled upward to what seemed forever. The large chandelier in the entrance cast dancing sparkles of light around the room. I removed my shoes and walked slowly onto the white marble floor.

"Come on in, would you like some rum and eggnog?" he said.

His family had gathered in the kitchen. They all stared intently at me with that familiar smile on their faces. We stood around the type of large island I had only seen in magazines. It was adorned with acorns and candle creations, and a spread of food such as I had never encountered.

I said to Neil, "I brought you something, a gift."

He said, "You really didn't have to do that."

I said, "This time I believe I do."

They all looked a bit confused as he unwrapped the paper. He stood silent as he held his old Bauer skates in his hands for the first time in twenty years.

I told him, as his eyes glazed once more, that these skates meant more to me then he could ever possibly fathom. My hands began to shake, and I swallowed hard. I bowed my head and shut my eyes as I cleaned the blackboard just one more time.

I regaled them with the tale of how his skates guided me not only down the ice but through my life. The lessons I had learned and unlearned. The experiences and sentiments I carried with me everywhere now. The feeling that I was chosen to receive the most important of messages.

I told them that feeling made up the infrastructure of my spirit, my First Nations identity. I had found my path and travelled that road, crossed that sea. Poetry still painted the pictures of my soul. The same way that I honoured and accepted my mom for her struggles through residential school and finding her own healing journey.

And now I'm telling you. My siblings all found their own path and they travelled it well. This is what sustains me.

Those lessons—that gift—gave me strength for the next thirty years. My children now are the best part of me, courageous and independent. The best Christmas gift ever helped me realize that acceptance of the people in your circle guarantees you the freedom to love. I am unwrapped a little bit each year—my memories, my experiences, the essence of who I am.

These are the skates that I give to you.

The Horse in the Desert

AVERILL GROENEVELD-MEIJER

I'm an adult woman, all grown-up with twenty-year-old children of my own, but my mother has died; I feel like a child, a drippy sad child, all over again.

Christmas approaches. Mom and I had so many together—she was a great, all-season granny to my kids, but especially so at Christmas, even though my earlier winter holidays as a child with divorced parents on different continents were more complicated.

Thinking of my mother at this time of year brings me back to when I was eleven years old or, more specifically, to what my mother remembered of the horse incident, which became a story she dined out on for decades. Now that she's gone, I will have to try to retell it for myself, this memory of a memory.

Picture dinner guests gathered around a table set with polished silver, crystal glasses, and fresh flowers. My mother has prepared three lovely courses that are matched with wines chosen by my stepfather. Guests mostly speak English, possibly some Dutch, and my mother launches this story—the horse in the desert—best in English, though it can also work in her rather elementary Dutch. My mother doesn't drink but she is merry, high on good company, basking in the soft glow of candles and fond friends.

My mother does not dwell on the background, which is that I am, as I mentioned, a sad child who is supposed to spend the break with my father and brothers in New York state as I'd done the previous two years. Instead, this year I have just been told that, for mysterious custody reasons, I must stay in The Hague and my older brothers must stay in Tuxedo Park, NY.

My memory has oddly done away with earlier Christmases when my parents were still together, but memories of the two I spent with just my dad and my brothers linger. Snow piled high in the yard and overwhelmed the crab apple trees beside the driveway. My father laced my skates the same way he braided my hair—as tightly as possible—for afternoons at the nearby lake. My brothers stayed up late waxing my skis, laid across the backs of the living room chairs, with Mom's old iron while they blasted that song I liked by The Who. The tree in the corner reached the ceiling and was decorated with dusty skeins of our grade-school crafts. Dad taught himself to cook a roast from *The Joy of Cooking*, but he swore as he tried to make gravy from scratch. There were parties with all the families in the neighbourhood, most of whom I had known since birth. Best of all, winter felt real, with snowstorms, sledding, and scarves, hats, and mittens.

It is unclear to me at eleven what Christmas in The Hague could look like. I haven't yet had one with just my mother and stepfather. The days are short and dark. The tall row house is cold and damp. My room under the eaves of the fourth floor attic is quiet, but for the rain clattering on the clay roof tiles overhead. The tree is small, set up on a table, and decorated with tiny white lights and hand-carved wooden ornaments from Germany. We don't know yet what we'll eat, nor when to open gifts. My mother and stepfather ask if I'd like to celebrate Sinterklaas at the same time as my Dutch classmates on December 5th or to hold off for the 25th for a more Christmassy feeling. Shoe or stocking? Gifts in the morning or evening? Turkey or wild game? I choose the 25th because it feels familiar, but part of me hopes I can have both.

As Sinterklaas approaches, we have a party at school with candy, poems, and a gift exchange. I give and receive a box of coloured pencils. Later, I put out my shoe for Sinterklaas, sing a few songs up the chimney, and leave out an apple for the Sint's grey horse. The next morning my shoe contains a chocolate letter "A" and a few marzipan fruits, which I am happy with until I get to school and hear all about the family parties and the funny gifts and poems my classmates received.

*

Worried that Christmas will be as bleak as my Sinterklaas, I decide to snoop. I wait for my mother and stepfather to go out and explore Mom's not-so-secret gift-hiding cupboard. Behind stacks of placemats and piles of old fabric, I find a shoebox tied shut with a bow. Shoes. I resign myself. Things look grim.

At school, the residual warmth and excitement around Sinterklaas fades. Craft projects veer toward winter and Jesus, incongruous snow scenes and hay mangers, but no Santa in sight. I long for New York state and draw mountains with colourful skiers and drifts of snowmen in bright scarves, with a shining star in the night sky leading the way, not to Bethlehem, but to Tuxedo Park and my dad. Outside the classroom windows, trees with bare branches reach into grey skies. After school, I walk home in the dark. I snivel all through the short, dreary days of December.

Ultimately, the poor weather, the drippy child, and certainly the distance from her sons, are all too depressing for Mom. My stepfather, at a loss, hopes to turn things around and books a last-minute trip to sunny Tunisia.

The plane flies through blue skies and lands in a shimmer of heat. The trees have lush green leaves and some even have oranges. The view from the shuttle bus window feels like a movie, with scenes I can barely comprehend: bicycles, cars, trucks weaving and honking; children running in and out of colourful shops; people leading donkeys and goats beside dusty roads.

Our hotel consists of a cluster of low-rise buildings laid out around a pool and surrounded by more palm trees and orange trees. A narrow path leads to the beach. Our rooms are on the second floor, down a long hallway with red and pink swirls on the carpet. It has been decided that I will have my own room, which is a bit frightening. There's no adjoining door, but apart from a utility closet, I'm right next to Mom and my stepfather's room.

Despite the promising start, the pool turns out to be too cold for swimming and the sea, while beautiful to look at, is much too rough. The second night, I'm woken up by a loud noise in the wall or maybe out in the hall. Metal clanks louder and louder. I want to call for Mom but I am too scared to leave my room. Just when I can't stand it anymore, Mom comes in and tells me my stepfather has called the front desk for help. A man arrives with a wrench. He opens the utility closet and bangs on some pipes until one of them cracks. Water hisses and pours down the hallway. The clanging noise problem resolved, the man leaves. Water continues to flood down the hall all night, soaking the length of the red and pink swirly carpet.

The next morning, my mother, stepfather, and I walk

out to look for a better hotel. Further down the beach, we come across a splendid modern resort with a huge heated pool. The lobby is big and white and shiny, but when my stepfather hears the rates he just shakes his head. Mom is disappointed. As we're leaving, we see that the fancy hotel even has its own stables. My stepfather is scared of horses, but he's trying to save the day. He enquires in French, and it turns out Mom and I are welcome to join a group going out for a ride along the beach, right away. The handsome stable manager, around Mom's age, looks at us and says he has two nice, quiet horses.

He doesn't know my mother was a real prairie girl who kept her very first pony (a mean little bastard, she says) beside her father's car in their garage on the outskirts of Calgary and that every couple of years, her pony was upgraded to something slightly less mean and more beautiful until she arrived at Jingles, the last and the best. Jingles was retired from the Mounties' musical ride and sometimes, when least expected, broke into fancy footwork reliving his past training.

Mom, though out of practice, is an expert rider. I have only had lessons for the past year, once per week in a group of eight, at a stable on the outskirts of The Hague. I can walk, trot, and canter around an indoor riding ring in ovals, circles, and diagonals, but when I stand beside horses in their narrow stalls trying to figure out how to bridle and saddle them, I

*

am secretly scared though I wish I weren't, because all I read are pony club books, British children's books that feature horse-loving girls with names like Jill and Ginny. The protagonists wear jodhpurs, jump their fat ponies over hedges at weekend gymkhanas, and muck out stalls early mornings before school. Oh, how I envy those girls.

The Tunisian stable manager asks no further details of our experience and hollers into the stables. A young groom leads out two calm-looking horses. Mom murmurs soothingly to each horse and says they look well cared for and suitably old. She chooses the grey mare for herself and nods at me to take the chestnut one. The stable manager gives me a knee up, mounts his own horse, and leads the group of horses and riders along the deserted beach. This is only my second trail ride.

The first time was on a sunny day in The Hague. Our instructor decided the horses deserved a treat. We left the stables in a long row and trotted along bridle paths into the North Sea dunes. It was something I'd always wanted to do and the day would have been a dream except my horse kept stopping to eat grass. His big rump blocked the way for the horses behind me and a traffic jam built up. Everyone was yelling at me to get my horse moving. I kicked and kicked but it was too busy tearing grass. The instructor had to tell a more experienced kid to ride beside me and hustle us along.

I felt defeated. I didn't know trail riding could be so hard. I thought it would be fun. Mom said later I hadn't been firm enough with the horse, and I was determined next time to do better.

Today is different. The horses spread out across the beach and walk along companionably. When the manager wants us to trot, he gives a shout and the horses break into a trot. When he wants us to canter, he shouts something else and we canter. There, under the Tunisian sun, sparkling waves on one side and rows of swaying trees on the other, I feel like I'm in control. I can relax—trail riding is actually fun. I feel I'm not such a bad rider after all.

As Mom tells it though, the horses are only doing exactly what the man is telling them to do. These horses, mom says, "Don't even dream of passing their leader at the front."

We return the horses and I skip down the beach. Christmas under the sun, no snow in sight, might be okay. We head back to our not very nice hotel while Mom tells my stepfather about how the horses are some kind of Arabian breed: showy, sleek, fast. She adds, "Those aren't just any old stable nags. They are so well trained you might not realize it, but those are desert horses. They can run forever."

Before the trip, I had been warned that Tunisians don't celebrate Christmas. Nevertheless, on Christmas Eve the hotel puts on a multi-course dinner of seafood. I pick at the shrimp cocktail and wrap the rest of the fish in napkins I hide on my lap under the tablecloth. I beg Mom for more stories about her horses and she tells of thrilling days galloping through the Prairies with her Irish setter by her side, and of lazy summer afternoons picking hundreds of ticks the size of blueberries off her horse.

She tells how the mean little ponies would buck her off miles from home and if she let go of the reins they would run home to their stables leaving her to walk back with just the setter for company. I take in the lesson. *Don't let go of the reins.*

I beg Mom and my stepfather for a horse of my own. A nice calm one to love and that will love me back, preferably brown with a black mane and tail, but any colour will do. They tell me of the impracticality of owning a horse in downtown The Hague, of the amount of time and money it would take. But I don't believe them. I'll never believe them.

I pause outside the restaurant. My mother and stepfather wander off hand-in-hand under yellow lights strung among trees. I sit on the hotel steps to feed leftovers to the stray cats I've seen skulking about. I call out, "Kitty, Kitty."

More and more cats show up to the feast; swarms of skinny cats with torn ears and fuzzy, striped kittens. They climb into my lap and onto my shoulders to get at the fish.

Hotel guests in fancy dress keep well to the other side of the stairs. The cats purr loudly and scratch me in the feeding frenzy, raising welts on my arms and legs. One tiny grey kitten has a huge lump above its eye. I hold it against my body and try to take it to Mom to see if she can help, but that kitten scratches and bites my bare arms and I have to let it go. I watch sadly as it scampers away in the dark.

When Mom includes the cats as an aside in her version of the story, she will tell of blood streaming down my face and staining my Liberty dress. Dinner guests will picture rivers of blood and wonder about tetanus shots, but I mostly remember being surrounded by the purrs of dozens of cats and that one little kitten I wanted to take home.

Christmas morning. I have already been told not to expect gifts, but that there will be a nice present waiting for when we get home. (I don't tell them I know it is shoes.) They also surprise me with another horse ride down the beach.

Mom and I walk along the beach to the stables. This time, the stable manager is not there. Instead, the young groom, older than me but younger than my brothers, brings out the same calm grey mare for Mom. The groom speaks little English but grasps my two hands in his and squeezes hard. He gazes into my eyes. I don't blink and squeeze back as hard as I can. I think we are testing my strength, whether

*

of hands or of will, I'm not sure. Or maybe he is just concerned about the scratches on my face and arms. Regardless, the groom nods, heads into the stables and returns, leading a shiny brown dream of a horse with a long black mane and tail. The horse pulls at his bridle, his eyes bright and ears perked forward as he poses for the other horses. His perfectly combed tail arches and swishes. I place a tentative hand on his smooth neck. His muscles tense briefly as his ears flick at a fly; there is little indication he even knows I am there.

"A real Arabian," Mom whispers in awe. She knows neither French nor Arabic, but she shakes her head and says loudly, "No, no, too much horse." She repeats herself louder. "Too. Much. Horse. That is too much horse."

The groom smiles, nods, and says, "*Oui, madame,* very good horse."

He gives me a boost into the saddle, fixes the stirrups, and tightens the girth.

I again pat the horse's neck gently, determined to show him how nice I am. I tell him bays are my favourite. He jumps sideways a bit, to show he is not impressed. But I'm pretty sure I can handle him, just like Ginny and Jill.

The ride starts out the same as before. The young groom takes the lead, and we walk along the deserted beach, again admiring the sun on the waves. We trot when he says to, then canter. The row of horses is ragged but they're still generally mannerly. They do not pass the groom.

He turns his mount, but not back down the beach to the hotel. Instead he heads inland through scrubby bushes and piles of trash toward the highway. He waves and yells at traffic until it stops and then leads us across the four lanes. My horse skitters on the pavement. My heart jumps. "It's just dancing," I tell myself. "Like Jingles from the musical ride."

My mother looks back to make sure I have crossed safely. She frowns. She's concerned. Worry creeping in, I grip the reins with my supposedly strong hands.

On the other side of the highway, the horses follow a sandy trail. There is a rusted chain-link fence on our left, but ahead and to the right is wide open space, just orange sand, scattered brush, and a few faded black tents in the distance belonging to Bedouins, I'm told. They herd sheep and goats and ride beautiful horses and maybe even keep camels, though the camp is much too far away to see if that's true.

Everyone, horses and riders, seem relaxed under the warm Tunisian sun. But not my horse, not me. I plant my feet more firmly in the stirrups, shift in the saddle, sit up straight, and lower my hands, teetering between the contentment of a Christmas day in the desert on a beautiful horse and an awareness that too much horse is going to be trouble.

*

The groom looks back at the column. He smiles and lets out a sudden blood curdling whoop as he sweeps his hand forward. All horses break.

My horse leaps forward. He is no longer content to be in the middle of the group. One by one he charges past the horses in front of us. The helmet I was wearing sails off my head. My heart stops, and restarts, only louder than before.

We pass my mother and she yells at me to slow down. I yank on the reins, my strong hands irrelevant once the horse gets the bit in his teeth. He seems to know he is gorgeous, that he is fast, and that he has no need for those in front of him, nor for this eleven-year-old on his back. I have never truly galloped before, but it turns out I know it when I see it. And so we gallop towards the groom who holds his arm out as if to catch my reins, but he misses and we race ahead.

The groom gives chase. My horse, my sleek Arabian steed, goes even faster. This is the fastest I have ever gone on my own, without the assistance of combustion or electricity, in my entire life to this day.

The speed is scary, but falling off will be worse. I concentrate on sticking on that horse's back. I try to recall everything Mom has ever told me about bastard ponies bucking her off in the prairie. Too bad that pony pair, Ginny or Jill, with their mystifying jodhpurs and gymkhanas, have never even seen a real Arabian horse. But I'm the rider. It's up to me, except I control neither direction nor speed. I push my heels down and grab onto the mane. Sometimes all you can do is hang on.

Mom will point out to her guests that his black mane and tail streamed in the wind, his flanks shone in the sun, as he raced into the distance taking no notice of her youngest child on his back. My senses are overwhelmed by the sound of pounding hooves. The world's an earthquake around me. I struggle to level my gaze between the horse's ears as taught in my first lessons back in The Hague. It beats looking down.

I fight to retain my balance and eventually discover something of an underlying rhythm to the horse's gait. Wind-tears stream down my face. I know Arabian horses are famous not just for speed but also for their endurance. Desert horses can run forever.

The desert seemingly has no real end, just orange sand dunes that fade into rust-coloured hills in the distance, hill upon hill. A strong horse with a lightweight rider could run forever and never get to the end.

But those faded black tents. We're getting close. I can see old men and young children moving around in front. My horse threatens to run right through that camp. Goats bleat. Children point. A white-bearded man wrapped up in a gown waves a crutch. Do I catch a glimpse of the gap in his teeth right before the horse shies away?

*

The groom takes that opportunity to come in from the side. He shouts and urges his horse on, forcing mine to turn in a wide arc back toward the sea. He screeches desperate pleas but my horse speeds up, still in a race, and keeps well ahead. This horse will never stop. My toes cramp around the stirrups. My legs ache. The strands of his mane cut my hands. Nevertheless, I keep hold at least as well as any Ginny or Jill.

We're approaching the highway. Trucks and buses honk on the road. My horse finds a gap in the traffic and he thinks he's going to make it until his hooves hit the asphalt and lose traction. We skid across the pavement, across four lanes of traffic squealing and honking. I lose the stirrups and wrap my arms around his neck.

The horse slows to a walk and releases the bit from his teeth. Sweat darkens his flanks. The groom catches up and dismounts. He peels the reins from my grip and walks us back and forth beside the highway while we wait for Mom and the others.

My mother's face is pale, her hands shake. She usually loves to laugh but she is not laughing. I'm hot and out of breath and sorry Mom is so worried, but all I can think is: take that Ginny, take that Jill.

The rest of the story is lost in my mother's hoots around the dinner table. Guests laugh into their excellent lemon soufflé. Mom delivers her punchline: "Like a peanut!! My precious angel, racing through the desert stuck like a small peanut on the back of the most magnificent horse you've ever seen."

And now my mother is dead and I am left with a story I can feel in my bones, in my fingers and toes, though I seem to have mislaid some of Mom's glorious embellishments. Perhaps I've added a few of my own. All I can do is fill in blanks she never knew.

I thought I was getting shoes for that Christmas. Instead, on the morning after we got back home, I sat on the edge of my mother and stepfather's bed. They handed me the shoebox. I opened it to find it filled with a family of miniature plastic horses. Five airbrushed bay horses nestled in newspaper.

We'll be short a person this Christmas dinner. But I will polish Mom's silver bowl. My husband will fill it with red roses and with the holly from the alley. I will cook all day: duck breast with Earl Grey tea sauce, wild rice from a box, and a lesser version of Mom's carrots and parsnips with orange, the original recipe long lost.

My stepdad will appear with a bottle of champagne and with Mom's little white dog in tow. I think we'll skip grace without Mom to say it, but we'll toast loved ones near, far,

*

departed. We'll dab our eyes. There might be moments of merry. We will snap crackers, wear paper hats at jaunty angles, and holler our riddles at the deaf Opa.

It's shocking to think that one day it might seem normal, because for now I am the weepy adult, the snivelly child, ageless in my grief.

Half-Empty

JENNIFER POWNALL

Dennis walked me down the aisle. More specifically, he met me and my father halfway along a stretch of white trellis and wove my arm through the crook in his before we continued between hundreds of fragrant blooms at the centre of the Stanley Park Rose Garden. He became a second dad to me at a time when my home life became rough, and he was one-fifth of the Emmett clan who had nurtured and challenged me in countless ways since I was thirteen.

All three Emmett siblings stood with us as we were married, Dylan acting as one of Evan's groomsmen, Joy as one of my bridesmaids, and Craig as the man-of-honour. The mom, Lynn, served in two roles that day. She was the emcee at our reception and—more importantly—she set off with Evan and me along a poorly trod path into the forest right after our public ceremony to officiate a private handfasting.

These people were not blood, but they had long past earned the title of family.

In Grade 8, Craig had brought me home like I was some eager, stringy-haired stray dog. I was polite enough to be accepted by Dennis and Lynn and sassy enough to be followed around by Joy, who was seven when we met.

Dylan was already graduating high school, so we didn't start hanging out for a couple of years. Overall, my slow, spiritual adoption as one of their own had no ritual to it. It was simply the inevitable conclusion of me showing up to every special occasion and all the little moments in between. I refused to go away. And for some reason, they embraced it. Joy was the first to call me sister, and eventually I became known as the "other daughter."

So, a couple years after our wedding, when Evan and I began trying for a baby and experiencing significant fertility issues, the Emmetts were with us in the trenches. When we found out we were pregnant for the first time and announced it at a dinner at their house, Lynn was the first to jump up and hug me. "You know," she said, "your dad is a twin! It runs in the family!"

"Oh," I said, hesitant to ruin the moment. "But, he's not actually my dad." Her face fell before I added, "But we have twins in our family too!" Lynn grinned and put her palms on my cheeks, squeezing my face affectionately. It was the first time I realized the divide between me and their other kids had truly disappeared. I was theirs. They were mine.

When that pregnancy came to an early end, Dennis sat at my bedside, patting my hand, his normal boisterous manner silenced to match my own. They were all there for me, as much as they could be. Their grief was an echo of Evan's and mine. Through two other failed pregnancies, followed by a couple of years of reproductive treatments, the Emmetts had felt the loss of promised nieces, nephews, and grandchildren as keenly as any blood relations could have. They brought me soup and cookies and magazines. They held space for me, both when I ranted and when I withdrew. They used up their birthday wishes on urging the universe to help Evan and me become parents. They kept us close, never missing an opportunity to bring celebration into our lives.

In 2013, when we moved into our first house at the beginning of January, we immediately began making plans to have them join us in our new home for Christmas. The Emmetts were well known for their yuletide festivities. They made three-dough neapolitan cookies that everybody grabbed as soon as they come out of the oven, stockings were filled with unfamiliar foodstuffs in individual Ziplocs, and, of course, there was teasing, fart jokes, and fuzzy onesie pyjamas with buttflaps that were occasionally left open. The wildness somehow seemed like the most honest reflection of love and joy.

Evan and I used their example of Christmases past to create our own version. We hung more decorations and lights than was necessary or even environmentally sound. We bought new stockings for everyone, even purchasing extras for the children we didn't yet have. We made certain we had a stockpile of decorative papers, tape, and a massive collection of ribbons and bows to support the Emmett tradition of finishing gifts at midnight and then panicking to get them wrapped.

It was a three-day affair. Joy and I baked shortbread, pinwheel cookies, snickerdoodles, and more. The small rooms of our Edwardian craftsman home were thick with the scents of cinnamon and butter, nutmeg and peppermint. Carols blared from speakers, and louder still was the mixture of laughter and swearing I had grown to expect over more than two decades of knowing these people. Evan took from Dennis' longstanding example of making stollen between unwrapping presents and rooting through stockings, and he started his own tradition of cooking waffles for everyone on Christmas morning. Our table overflowed with jams, whipped cream, maple syrup, berries, and homemade apple butter.

I brought out acrylic and wooden ornaments in the shape of gingerbread people and made a huge production of getting everyone to craft their own. The boys painted childhood cartoon characters, Lynn made a stunning abstract gold and red mosaic, and Joy turned hers into a masked wrestler, complete with a miniature barbell hoisted over his shoulder which she fashioned out of part of a skewer and couple spare jingle bells. Dennis gave his a butthole.

It was the perfect Christmas.

And then it was over, and Evan and I returned to the normal grind of life, slightly buoyed by the memory of that first Christmas in our home as we continued with fertility treatments and the accompanying cycles of hope and dis-appointment. The better part of a year passed, and as we began to look forward to repeating the fun and chaos we had created during the holidays, we also started to consider what our lives would be like if I was not able to have children.

We contemplated a life without kids but knew that was not what we wanted. We talked about surrogacy, though Evan thought it would be too hard on me to watch some-one else carry our baby. We discussed fostering children instead of seeking to expand our family more permanently, but we were confident that path would leave us heartbroken from the inevitable goodbyes. Finally, we broached the topic of adoption.

It felt right. My mom had lost her mother at the age of three and had gone to live with her maternal aunt. Her being raised in that way felt like an adoption story to me. Dennis found out after his dad had passed that he was not his biological father, a fact his dad had known from the beginning, though he never let the lack of a blood tie define his relationship with his son. My personal experiences with being totally embraced by the Emmetts as one of their own had long felt like a sort of adoption. But I worried about one thing.

Would I love an adopted child as much as I would love one I had birthed?

It seemed wrong to adopt a child if we were not able

to love it as fully as one with genetic ties. I started to ask people about their thoughts and feelings on the subject, and I often felt both selfish and righteous in exploring the question. We wanted to do right by any kid we might potentially bring into our home. We didn't want to build our family on half-hearted attachments.

Of course, our intuition told us from the beginning that we were worrying for no reason. It seemed obvious we would love them the same. The very first time I had asked the question out loud, Evan looked at me with equal parts reassurance and confusion.

He replied, "We would love them because they would be ours."

My husband is far less inclined than I am to haul an anxiety around, and he was fast to reiterate the same conclusion, even after my relentless barrage of "what if's". But even as we strung coloured lights along our eaves and I prepped holiday cards with wishes for a wonderful upcoming 2015, I was unsettled. I had initially been seeking guidance from those slightly removed from our closest circle of friends and family. Everyone had been through so much as we went along our complicated journey to parenthood, and I had not wanted to start raising hopes of a new possibility until I was more confident in how I felt about it. But the need to gather more data won out over my reservations.

A couple of weeks before Christmas, I went to Dennis

and Lynn's house to ask them about why they thought of me as their other daughter. Sitting at their dining room table was a moment of double apprehension for me. Not only was I trying to subtly determine their opinion on whether I might be able to fully love an adopted child, but I was also opening myself up to the risk of them admitting their affection for me was less than that they held for their own kids, or at the very least different.

I asked if the moniker of daughter was sincere and if they really believed I was a part of the family. We talked a lot about how I came into the clan and Dennis laughed, saying, "You just kept showing up!"

I finally quit dancing around what I wanted to know and asked, "Do you love me the same as the others?"

Lynn reached across the walnut tabletop and took my hand, staring hard into my eyes. "Of course," she said firmly.

Dennis smiled, nodding. "You pushed your way into this family. I don't think it matters where the relationship starts, but rather how it develops and where it ends up."

Christmas came and went, slightly more subdued than the previous year, and the Emmetts celebrated at our place again. Dylan had plans with his in-laws, but Craig and Joy stayed the night. Dennis and Lynn had booked a hotel to avoid our pull-out sofa, but they were back before ten on Boxing Day morning. Evan had to work, and because the

✳

buses were running less frequently due to the holiday schedule, asked if we could pick him up part-way along his route home in the evening. Joy and I volunteered to go.

That night we hopped into her pickup truck, our bellies bulging with day-old waffles and hot chocolate, and chatted about how relaxing the day had been. We complained about our full stomachs and groaned when the seatbelts cut into them in the corners but laughed as we talked about how loud my small house seemed at this time of year, even without any children in it.

Joy drove carefully amidst the scattered traffic of homeward bound deal hunters. "I wonder if Dylan will have kids."

"I don't know," I replied. "Him and Danielle don't ever talk about it."

"Yeah," she trailed off. She was quiet for a moment and then said, "I think he wants kids."

I shrugged. "I'm not sure Danielle does."

"But shouldn't he have a say in that?" Joy asked.

I looked at her, my skin prickling at her seeming annoyance, and then I let my gaze skip back to the road in front of us. "Yes," I said. "I'm sure he does. It's not the sort of thing you just ignore. They've been married a few years. I'm sure they've talked about it."

"I doubt it," Joy said.

I shook my head involuntarily. "Dylan is capable of saying what he wants."

Joy snorted. "Are you serious? When he was a kid he lied all the time."

"Well," I said, "he just turned forty, so I think he'd be capable of talking honestly to his wife if he wants kids."

"You don't know him like I do," Joy said. "You're not part of the family."

One heartbeat. That was all I felt before fire skyrocketed from the bottoms of my feet, travelled up my spine, and raced over the top of my head to settle like an inferno in my cheeks. "Let me out." The words sounded ragged through my clenched teeth.

She looked over at me. "What? Why?"

"Let me the fuck out," I managed to spit out each word individually.

Joy signalled and pulled the truck over. The warm glow of Christmas bulbs hanging from trees lining the street blurred into a thick, grotesque snake of light hovering above the passing traffic. I was shaking as I fumbled for the handle, and when I found it, I yanked on it and spilled out onto the sidewalk. I slammed the door and began walking. Instinctively, I had turned back in the direction from which we had come. I strode without seeing anything for about two blocks before I took a real breath and felt the night air stirring cool against my skin. I blinked against the welling sensation behind my eyes.

How could she say I wasn't a part of the family? How

dare she tell me I hadn't fully earned the mantle of honorary Emmett? I was as much a part of the family as she was. I started coming around when she was seven! Dylan was ten years older than her, so does he have more of a right to be considered family than she does? Of course not! So why does she get to tell me I'm not a part of it? Because I'm not blood? What does that matter?

But it mattered. It mattered enough for her to make a distinction. And if she was able to see a difference—feel a difference—then maybe there was a difference. Maybe I wasn't actually her sister. And maybe if I adopted a child, I would never fully consider them mine.

The walk home took me over an hour. My thoughts oscillated from fixating on the rejection I felt when I got out of the truck to inventing conversations with Evan where we would be forced to decide against adoption. I thought about the children I had started to imagine could be with us by next Christmas. I wondered if Evan had been picked up, if Joy had told everyone what had happened, and if I could get away with walking straight into my room and going to sleep when I got back. My stomach lurched with every new contemplation and my cheeks felt stiff from layers of dried tears.

When I was finally walking along the last few blocks toward my house, I knew I wasn't ready to deal with what had happened. I was still in the thick of feeling everything and I had no words to answer the barrage of questions I was certain I was about to face. I walked down the alley behind my home instead of approaching from the front. I assumed people might be watching for me. The enormous spruce in our backyard was lit up with hundreds of red bulbs we had wrestled into its branches with an extendable pole from atop a ladder, and its hulking silhouette was both beautiful and terrible.

Had I ruined Christmas?

I walked around the side and slipped through the gap in the fence. The sensor light clicked on, and from a few feet away I peered through the window in the top portion of our back door, holding my breath. Nobody came down the stairs to investigate. I sighed and sat down on the hard brick stoop.

I was there for an hour. My mind continued to invent arguments and speeches and discussions, and anger seeped back in when I thought about how no one had gone out looking for me. Didn't anyone care that I was missing?

Finally, the door inside at the top of the stairs opened and shut and I heard footsteps come down the narrow steps. Relief and annoyance fought inside my chest. Craig's face appeared in the window. He opened the door.

"What are you doing?" He was incredulous, but as his eyes adjusted to the night and my dishevelled state registered, his face and tone softened. "What's going on?"

He sat down beside me and put an arm over my shoulder.

I shook my head, any explanation I might offer crouching thick around the base of my tongue.

"Joy said you had a fight, but she doesn't know what happened."

I huffed. "She knows exactly what happened."

"Okay," he said, "then come upstairs and let's talk about it."

I shook my head again. "I don't think that's a good idea."

Craig stood up and held his hand out. "It's Christmas. Let's sort this out."

I sighed and let him pull me up. The numbness in my rear tingled as I unfolded my body from the cold porch step. "I feel like this is going to be bad. I'm not ready to talk to her."

"Don't make me be the mature one," Craig said. "We both know that never works out."

I plodded up the stairs behind him, and Evan met us at the top. He handed me a wineglass half filled with Moscato and gave me a hug.

"I'm not ready to talk about this," I whispered to him, my anxiety ebbing slightly as I leaned into his tall, warm frame. Old Spice and hazelnut coffee filled my nose.

"You'll do great," he reassured me, and for a moment I believed him. I also took a big gulp of the sweet, sparkling alcohol.

Dennis sat down at the dining room table between Joy and me, clearly prepared to mediate. Craig disappeared back downstairs to our guest room, and Lynn and Evan settled onto our purple couch in the adjoining living room, a looping video of a yule log burning in a fireplace playing on the television in the corner.

"Alright. Let's sort this out," Dennis began. He looked expectantly from me to Joy.

"I don't understand what happened," Joy said, her shoulders rising slightly.

I focused on keeping every muscle in my face still.

"We were just talking," she continued. "What did I say?"

I snorted and drank the last of the wine down in several large mouthfuls. "It doesn't matter," I said evenly.

Dennis leaned toward me. "JenPow," he said expectantly. The affectionate nickname caught me off guard and sliced through the tenuous control I was struggling to hold onto.

"I can't talk about this right now," I replied. My voice was thick with the emotion I tried to smother.

"All I said is that you weren't around when we were growing up," Joy said. My gaze snapped to her, and the shaky breath I had been drawing was replaced by an audible expulsion of air as my mouth dropped open and an imperceptible sneer formed in front of my grinding teeth. "It's true," she said, not sensing the danger.

"That is not what you said." I didn't recognize my own voice.

"We were talking about Dylan, and I said you weren't a part of the family when we were all kids," she said, "and then you got out of the truck."

I stared at her, dumbfounded. "Are you serious?"

"Are you mad because I said you don't know Dylan like I do?"

"I am furious because you said I am not a part of this family."

"I just meant you weren't when we were kids!"

"But that's not what you fucking said!" I screamed, standing up. The tiniest flicker of reason registered before I threw the glass I was clutching, and the thing smashed against the bottom of the wall to my right, the last drops of wine spraying in all directions to dot the long, floral curtain and the worn, century-old hardwood.

"Get out of my fucking house!" I yelled. Joy was on her feet and pushing past me to leave before I finished my demand. Evan suddenly filled my vision and I started sobbing as he wrapped one strong arm around me and pulled me past the large table and under the glittering red tinsel garland hanging above our bedroom door. I pushed away from him, gasping, my heart thudding against the inside of my chest.

"I want to go. I want to go now." I heard Lynn say to Dennis. "You don't treat family like that."

All of my rage drained away. I could hear them gathering up their things in the next room. "Lynn?" I called out, hoarsely. "Lynn?" I said again when there was no response. I stepped back into the main part of our house as she was crossing through the dining room.

*

She held up one shaking hand, her eyes red and glistening. "I have to go," she said quietly.

"I'm so sorry," I blubbered. "Lynn, I am so sorry. I don't know what happened. I said I wasn't ready to talk. I knew I shouldn't, but—" I broke off, unable to speak past my tears.

She walked past me to retrieve her purse and coat from the low chest by our front door and I followed. "Please," I tried again, "I don't know why I did that. I was so angry, but I shouldn't have—"

Lynn turned to face me, holding her crimson jacket tight against her body. "I love you," she said, "but I have to go. I have to make sure she's okay."

I nodded silently, as she and Dennis slipped their shoes on and left. The glow from the Christmas tree behind me cast coloured bits of light against the closed door, and I heard Evan collect the broom and dustpan from our kitchen before the rhythmic rustle of bristles against floor told me he had begun to sweep up the shards of broken glass.

It took a year—and a single moment—to heal the relationship between Joy and me.

I worked through things with the rest of the family quickly. Lynn, in particular, was more gracious than I deserved. I shared my side of the events at first, living in the rejection and refusing to see where I had gone wrong. The Emmetts and Evan listened and acknowledged my pain, but offered enough gentle prompting for me to start thinking more critically about what had happened. Eventually I was able to look back at that night with the intention of understanding where the breakdown had occurred. For the first time, I saw clearly the intense vulnerability that had been built up from years of infertility. I had used how close the Emmetts and I had been to validate my assumptions about how I would feel if we adopted a child. I wanted to love them without barriers, to know they were truly mine no matter how they came into the world. But when Joy said what she said I was crushed. It undermined my understanding of my place in their clan—of anyone's place in a family they are not born into—and it made me doubt everything.

Anger faded to embarrassment. Months later, I began asking how Joy was doing, though I was too ashamed to reach out to her directly.

Evan and I moved forward with our plans to research adoption. We went through orientations and took classes, read books and articles, and met with representatives from both private and public agencies. We looked into international options and considered where we stood in regards to older and multiple adoptions. We educated ourselves on the terms "open" versus "closed" and why the latter rarely exists anymore, and we set up meetings with people who had actually adopted children of their own so we could hear about their firsthand experiences.

Then, one night in September, an epiphany cut through the mountain of information we had gathered. We realized that if we had all the money in the world we would have already adopted. The only thing holding us back was our concern over financial resources. The hesitation had nothing to do with our capacity to welcome a child as our own. It had nothing to do with love.

That set us free. We were positive we would adopt. The one element keeping us from immediately moving forward was the two embryos we still had frozen with our reproductive clinic. Adoption protocols ask prospective parents to have completed any fertility treatments prior to beginning the application process to ensure commitment. We set up our final appointment to transfer the last of our genetic material into my uterus, certain an implantation would never occur.

But one did.

I found myself in late November rapping briefly at the entrance of the Emmetts before I lifted the latch and let myself in. Ever committed to the oncoming season, a vertical line of red and white felt Santas swung from the back of the door as I closed it. Boxes of ornaments and lights had already been pulled from their crawlspace to line the hallway and spill into the living room. A two-foot artificial tree was lit up on one end table, and tossed onto another was a hat that, when worn, looked like the rear end of a cooked turkey.

Empty cookie tins littered their kitchen counters, and I spied the stained copy of Dennis' stollen recipe on my way out to the back porch.

Lynn was sitting outside reading, and she gave a happy, "Oh! Hi!" as I came through the sliding glass door. I grinned at her and immediately went to unzip my hoodie.

"Hi!" I said, thrusting my stomach out in an exaggerated way. She looked at me, confusion and amusement clear in her face, until she saw the bright yellow Baby on Board sign I had taped to my belly.

"Oh." She jumped up and hugged me tightly. Her hands made quick, small circles on my back as she giggled and bounced up and down.

"Really?" she asked, pulling back for a moment to touch the piece of paper.

Her smile was enormous as I said, "Really."

Her brown irises danced, but then they skipped past me to rest above my left shoulder. I turned around and there was Joy. We locked eyes for a moment. Then I smiled and pointed at my stomach. She looked down and back up, her mouth open in amazement, and stepped forward to gather me in a hug.

We stood there holding one another and crying for a long time.

It took a couple of conversations to talk everything through, but the pregnancy simplified things. Welcoming a child—whether through adoption or birth or any of the other ways children become a part of our lives—is supposed to be about beginnings. For me, it served to uncomplicate my relationships and offer a way into love that was free of labels, less burdened by my own insecurities about whether I had earned my place within my found family.

We walk together. We stand together. We offer ceremony and ritual to the special moments of our lives, and we find one another when we are lost. We experience elation and grief as if they are our own. We offer simple comforts and show up for the big moments, laughing and hollering in equal measure. We see one another through crucial decisions, give reassurance of the places we have in each other's lives, and then allow misunderstanding to break our collective hearts. We are the cut and the balm. We are family. And that is something worth celebrating all year long.

Arviat

LILLIAN AU

Frank and I were grounded at the airport in Rankin Inlet on our way from Yellowknife to Arviat. Flying up north was always dicey in the dead of winter. The delays piled on: dense fog, blowing snow, poor visibility, and a missed connection. Our layover dragged into the next day. We thought we were finally heading out when the latest flight was cancelled. There wasn't enough crew to staff the plane.

I should have known better than to travel the week before Christmas. Part of my job anchoring a TV news show in Yellowknife included reading the weather. For up to six months of the year, I would trot out the forecast, a predictable spiel: icy conditions, freezing drizzle, heavy snowfall, blizzard, and white-out. Sometimes, when it was -35°C, I didn't even bother saying the minus part. It was a given— just like being delayed by adverse weather.

It felt like I was stuck forever alone in the hotel room while Frank, who was a politician, headed out for impromptu meetings. I counted four mothballs underneath the bed. The room had a deep, shut-in smell. It needed to be aired out. It reminded me of the correctional facility in Yellowknife where we used to visit inmates from Arviat as part of Frank's job.

I did a couple of laps around the room trying to kill time. I watched *M*A*S*H* in Inuktitut. I stared out the window. It overlooked a bogged-down snowplough. Footsteps in the snow weaved from the machine in the direction of the town's liquor store (unlike Arviat, Rankin didn't have a booze ban). Perhaps the driver had called it quits and walked away. I tried to open the window but it was frozen shut. It would have to wait until spring for the ice to thaw to slide open again.

After each cancellation and return to the suite, I had to unpack the perishables in my luggage and put them in the hotel mini-bar fridge: the ice packs, o-j, a block of cheese, a pint of strawberries, a gallon of milk, and a chub of bologna that Frank liked. Food prices were inflated in Arviat so you had to bring your own or pay through the nose.

In another baggage piece, I had stuffed between the wool socks and thermal long johns two bottles of Captain Morgan's spiced rum, enough to last Frank through the holiday. Booze was contraband. Arviat was a dry community. Frank made sure it was shoved in my luggage. It wouldn't look good if the Member of the Legislature for Arviat got caught smuggling.

I also had to deal with a giant Rubbermaid tub with a broken lid held by duct tape. It contained donation items— used clothing, books, pairs of prescription glasses, sports equipment, and toys. The heaviest was the sewing machine, my mother's. It had an off-white hard case with a handle and metal clasps that closed neatly with a decisive snap. I used to brush my fingers over the nubbly surface. I nicknamed it "Turtle."

For years, Turtle hid in my mother's closet in the East Vancouver special where I grew up. It was tucked under the sweeping rows of dresses, flared pants, flowery blouses, and crocheted cardigans. The type of clothes you would freeze in if you wore them in Arviat in December. I guess I was eight years old, or maybe ten, when I discovered it. I liked to snoop around in my parent's bedroom out of boredom, looking for spare change, and my mother liked to hide envelopes of cash in the closet. My parents had secrets. A nosy kid, I wanted to unlock them. I guess that's why I became a journalist.

I tried to piece together why my mother had Turtle in the closet when she had a perfectly good Singer sewing machine with a fold-out table smack in the middle of the room, taking a place of more importance than the bed. I really identified that Singer with my mother. She was a heavy-duty sewing machine operator in a factory. Turtle was newer, untouched, still in its box. Why didn't she bring it out? The Singer was pretty old. Was it for me? I found out why one day. After one of her blowouts with my father, my mother sat on the bed alone, crying. In a burst of anger, she blurted out that my father bought Turtle for someone else. I knew my father cheated with other women. And I could guess whom my mother meant.

Turtle never got a chance to sew. No patches, no let-out side seams, not even hemmed cuffs. It never mended the unravelled or frayed. It took up space in the closet and in the back of my mind. When my mother could no longer see the width of a thread, and the straight stitch lines started to blur and zigzag, she retired from her job. By that time, my father had opened a printing shop and she joined him at the store in labour but not love. The business specialized in making ornate red Chinese wedding cards. The words between them to forgive, to move on, were left unspoken as they hot-stamped in gold foil on cardstock embossed with hearts and celebratory characters for double happiness, devotion, and joy.

When I grew up and moved out of the house, I went north to work as a broadcast journalist. I would still come down regularly to visit my parents. The house was unchanged except my father replaced the old Zenith TV with sixty-inch-screen Sony so he could see better from his La-Z-Boy chair. Stacks of newspapers, the latest software manuals in their boxes, and gadgets you would buy late at night lined the walls. When dementia took hold of my mother, Turtle was still in the closet. I would go to the dump in South Vancouver to declutter the house. But I kept Turtle.

I thought about tossing it out on the curb or dropping it in the donation bin of the Value Village on Victoria Drive, but I couldn't make myself do it. I didn't want this sewing machine in someone else's hands if that someone could be that woman. It never crossed my mind that she was probably already dead. And if she was still alive, could she even sew?

I suppose I wanted Turtle to escape the scene of the crime. I lugged it up north to Frank's place, a little bungalow. When Frank announced we were going to spend Christmas in Arviat, I thought, "Perfect opportunity," and also, "Not again."

My first visits to Arviat were periods of discovery. I marvelled at how close-knit the community was, the beauty of the land, and its rich Inuit way of life. After the fifth trip, the novelty wore off. I was a die-hard Southerner. I liked swimming at Kitsilano's outdoor pool, buying shoes from Gravity Pope, and my bubble teas with thirty percent sugar and fifty percent less ice. Up north, I always missed eating dim sum. Plus the isolation of staying in such a remote community was hard to get used to. Arviat would never be my first choice for Christmas break. I would have preferred to blow my northern allowance by jetting down and drenching myself in sunshine and warmth.

Frank had said, "You know it's an election year coming up. I have to be seen."

I told him people had better things to do than have Frank in their face during the holidays. Maybe they deserved some space.

"Don't be difficult. If I'm not there, I'm out of their mind. With less than eight hundred people voting last time, I need every single vote. This really matters."

*

I knew what he meant. Every year, Arviat threw itself into a holiday feast at the John Ollie Hall to celebrate the season, to lift up the community from the darkness of deep winter, and to share the bounty of the land. Frank knew, and I did too, that everyone would be there and if you were a politician, it was necessary to attend.

He paused and switched gears. He was good at talking in soundbites and swaying people. "After the election we'll go somewhere warmer. Just be . . . patient."

I was patient. I was pushing way past thirty, engaged to Frank for four years, creeping into five, with no wedding date set. That said, neither of us seemed to be in a hurry to take the next step. Our relationship drifted along year after year. It's true, my job took a back seat to Frank's career. I stopped covering the legislature as a television reporter because it would have been a conflict of interest. I ended up doing fluff stories about carvers building ice castles on Yellowknife Bay and dog sled races during Caribou Carnival. My engagement ring went missing when we went camping somewhere near the Thelon River, where the wild herds migrated up and down the tundra. I didn't feel an urgent need to replace it even though I felt bad about losing such an expensive rock. At night, it used to stare back at me like a high beam coming from the headlights of a semi about to run me down.

It was always easier to go along than make a fuss about

most things with Frank. Any relationship was a series of compromises, right? I didn't like plastering a fake smile on my face when Frank was on public duty, but it was what I had to put up with to be with him. It was nothing compared to what my mother had to live with.

"We can go to the dump," Frank continued. "You're bound to see some polar bears."

Going to the dump was a thing up north. However, the one in Arviat was nothing like Yellowknife. The locals called it YKEA and bragged that it was better than IKEA. I did like going there to scavenge for treasures. It's where I found a fifteen-pound dumbbell and a half-dead fig plant. Once, my prospector friend found giant stuffed polar bears and unshredded government documents and wrote about it. God, I wish it had been me.

The dump in Arviat was smaller, had fewer consumer items in good condition, and more straight-up garbage. Plus the bears were the real deal. They would come off Hudson Bay searching for food, all skinny and bony looking. It was taking longer for the water to freeze and harder for the bears to hunt. It was both a sad and scary spectacle to watch people on ATVs dodging the starving polar bears. My heart broke when I saw them eating diapers.

Frank squeezed my hand and made a last-minute sales pitch. "This trip is long overdue. I have to spend time here with the constituents. Lots of stuff to catch up on. It'll be a few days of visiting and cups of tea. They won't bother us after Christmas. Everything slows down. We can relax and chill. Enjoy our one-on-one time together. No pressure."

We finally got the call from the Rankin Inlet airport that the weather was letting up.

"*Taima*!" Frank yelled in relief.

We packed our bags, I emptied the fridge once again, and we took off toward the airport. I tried to embrace what was ahead: drinking cups of Earl Grey tea with strangers in their home. These quick constituent visits would stretch to one or two hours at the kitchen table with multiple pit stops to the toilet. I would be fulfilling my duty. I would be showing loyalty. I would be a good partner. He needed support, and I would be there. Not like my father.

Above the clouds, the drone of the plane's motor accompanied the soft murmurs of Inuktitut in the cabin. Frank catnapped beside me, his mouth finally set on silent mode.

He was like my father in that way. Frank charmed his way into people's hearts despite being a *quallunaaq* and not speaking the language. He liked to sprinkle his thank-yous in Inuktitut by adding much to it. It's hard to stay mad at someone who finished everything with a "*mashi* much." That was Frank. He made you feel good. I fell for the same spell. I loved his wit and self-deprecating humour. He was everything I wasn't. Wasn't it fun to bask in so much of his glory?

Forty minutes into the flight, the plane started its descent. I looked down at the blocks of ice floating on Hudson Bay. They looked like missing pieces of a jigsaw puzzle. A hundred kilometres north of the tree line, Arviat sat in an ice-covered landscape and seascape that stretched endlessly. No roads connected it to another town. Frank was still sleeping when the spoilers folded down. I picked up one of my polar bear mitts. The fur on the mitts was oily and coarse. They were the most uncomfortable mitts I had ever worn. They swallowed my hands and were too unwieldy to grasp anything small. They were a gift from Frank. I tickled his nose and he scrunched his face up.

The plane hit the ground hard, skidded, and bumped along the ice and gravel until it rolled to a stop. The doors opened and the brittle air punched my face. I threw my hood up. My lungs clenched as I sucked in the cold. In my Sorels, I clunked my way down the narrow metal stairs and headed towards the terminal. The airport had no control tower, just a squat building in need of a paint job. After a brief wait, the Rubbermaid box was dumped on the airport floor.

The dog kennel arrived last. It was Qimmiq, Frank's dog. He smelled of pee and misery. Qimmiq meant dog in Inuktitut. He had been cooped up in his kennel since boarding in Yellowknife. His hair was matted and he looked defeated. Part husky and malamute, Qimmiq was a stray that had followed Frank to his hotel during a snowstorm in Tuktoyaktuk.

When Qimmiq spotted us, he started clawing at the cage door. He had a bug-eyed look of relief and desperation. I lifted the latch and opened the door to give him a hug. He tried to bolt. I grabbed his collar to stop him from running to the exit but, looking back, maybe I should have let him go.

The snow sprawled on the land with a voluptuous abandon. Our cab inched its way to Frank's Arviat house, a modest wooden building perched on blocks. Heavy drifts piled up against it. The cabbie unloaded our luggage on the side of the road and took off. Frank started to wade into a waist-deep layer of snow toward the house.

"Knuckleheads." Frank meant Joey, his constituency assistant, whose job it was to check on the house, and the kid Joey hired to clear the path every once in a while. It had been more than a while. Frank breaststroked through the snow to reach the door. He jiggled the knob back and forth. It didn't give. Thick ice encased the door frame.

"Mary, Jesus, Joseph! I can't believe this is happening! Let's see if the neighbours are home. Wait here. I won't be long."

I tried to carve a proper path to the street in the snow with my boots just to keep moving. Frank came back with a hammer. After a couple of minutes chipping away at the ice he tried the doorknob. No luck.

"What a piece of crap. Christ Almighty!"

"This was your idea to come here. Why couldn't we stay in Yellowknife?" I admit I whined unhelpfully.

Frank headed back to the neighbour's house and returned with a pry bar. He wedged the bar where the dead bolt connected to the frame and shoved hard. The wood cracked and split open. The door knob snapped off. He kept pushing until the door gave way. Frank said, "Satisfied?"

"Good job breaking in."

The house was as welcoming as a walk-in freezer. Our breath hung in the air like idling exhaust from the tailpipe of a car. A cold wind blasted through the hole where the doorknob used to be. I took off a boot and peeled a sock off. I gave it to Frank and he plugged it. We kept our parkas on the first night.

The next day I knew Frank had to catch up on meetings that were delayed by the storm but I slept in. When I woke up I was alone. Frank most likely had gone to his constituency office to get stuff done before things completely shut down for Christmas.

I started to unpack the luggage. The food was already stashed in the refrigerator even though I could have simply left it outside where it was colder. Frank had warned me on my first visit not to do that. Polar bears. After the clothes,

71

I moved on to the Rubbermaid. I flipped the lid open and removed the sewing machine.

The past jumped out at me. I can only guess I was less than ten years old. It was something that had stuck with me. I don't know why, maybe because my mother was driving and she didn't drive a lot.

There's condensation on the passenger window. I see rain falling on a tree-lined street in Strathcona, next to Chinatown. Wipers squeak back and forth. I sit in the back of a car drawing on the foggy window with my index finger. My mother stares out the windshield. It's a game. We're playing hide and seek. She is spying on my father. I like spending time with my mother. She is always working. But what is the point of it? What are we doing here? A gloom sets in. She is crying. The rain and tears run together.

I decided to leave the machine in the Rubbermaid. There was nowhere to put it. I didn't want to deal with it. I turned on the radio to fill the silence. On the airwaves, Christmas greetings volleyed back and forth. It was a holiday tradition to exchange well-wishes with friends and loved ones across the north. *Quviasugattaritti* ("may there be happiness in your lives") echoed in my ear. I let the rolling cadence of Inuktitut wash over me. The suicide rate in Nunavut is the highest in Canada but you wouldn't know it. People were good at hiding their feelings and pretending everything was alright. After twenty minutes, I couldn't keep listening but there was no internet, cell phone service, or TV. I had the urge to go out and get away from my thoughts. I thought I would hit the Northern Store, my usual first stop when I came to Arviat.

The wind drilled into my face. Crusty ice and frost coated my eyelashes and nose hair. It was -40°C outside. A perfect, blank layer of snow swaddled the land. The bottom layer of snow was like concrete but the top was soft like cotton candy. I waddled to the store.

Under the four layers of clothing I was wearing I could have had a supermodel body but you wouldn't know it. Still, any local normally could spot a Southerner because they often wore Canada Goose parkas. They were the uniform of folks who moved up to Yellowknife. Really warm, really expensive, but if you went to a house party and dumped it on the bed of the host, good luck finding yours at the end. I hated them.

In Arviat, the local Inuit proudly wore handmade parkas made of wool, canvas, brightly patterned calico, poly-ester-cotton poplin called Commander, and quilted batting called Hollofil. Each had their own look. Most of the boys had the numbers of their favourite hockey player and team logo sewn on. My first real northern coat was a hand-me-down. It was a man's and off its hood hung wolverine paws. I used to lift them and wave the claws like Happy Cat but the paw joke wore out. I now wore a bright orange, Arviat-styled one. The hood was trimmed with rabbit fur and the cuffs and hem were detailed with rickrack ribbon.

It was a warmer parka but on the land that day I felt raw and exposed. Qimmiq trotted ahead and I followed his footsteps. A chorus of Ski-Doo and ATV engines screamed in the icy air. A 4x4 driver with a cigarette hanging from his mouth gave me a nod as he cruised by. A kid sat on his lap, a woman sat behind with a baby in the back of her *amauti*, and another child dangled somehow like a circus acrobat.

I continued to slog toward the Northern Store. Qimmiq was in paradise. He zigzagged, sniffing everything, marking everything. I'm not sure if he followed me or I followed him to the bright blue sign. It was a plain one-storey warehouse with corrugated siding. I took out the leash. I chased him around a bit and clipped him in. I tied Qimmiq to a ramp railing.

I savoured the warmth inside. I checked out the price of items. I spied a seven-dollar bottle of China Lily soy sauce, a brand most Chinese people wouldn't be caught dead using because of its sweet-syrupy-goopy taste. If you dipped frozen arctic char in it, it was a delicacy equal to sushi. I put the bottle back on the shelf, but I really wanted to buy something.

I liked shopping. When I went down to Vancouver, I'd buy block-heeled designer shoes that I couldn't wear in Yellowknife most of the time. On camera as an anchor, it was the top that counted. No one saw below. So I didn't bother wearing them at work. Plus I had flat feet and a bunion. It made no sense. I made no sense.

I wandered to the back. The sharp scent of evergreen hit my nose. There were real honest-to-God trees on display, real ones wrapped tightly in a mesh straitjacket. Obviously flown in from down south. Usually, the closest thing with a trunk and branches were eight-dollar heads of broccoli. I stared at them.

I don't know what came over me. I wanted a real tree. I hated the ugly artificial ones I grew up with. Before he became a printer, my father worked at a sawmill cutting shingles and the last thing he wanted during the winter break was to smell fresh-cut wood. Even as a small child, I had a complicated relationship with him. He was a lousy husband but he was an okay father. He made sure we had food on the table and all that, and I'll never forget the time when he was on strike and he took me on the picket line outside the mill. I held his scarred hand which was missing two inches from his pinkie. And there was that smell of cedar.

Even though it was a rip-off, I walked over to the cashier to pay for a six-foot tall balsam. It was $200. And I had a plan. In my mind, I had a vision of Qimmiq, back on the land, doing what he was bred to do, following his instinct to run, to sled, to haul the tree home.

I got some rope, made a crude tie around the mesh and attached the other end to his harness. Qimmiq's furry ears perked up. His eyes lit. He began to jump and turn on the spot. It was time for Qimmiq to do his thing. I said something to the effect, "C'mon, Qimmiq, let's get this thing home."

He wouldn't budge.

I said, "Mush." Go straight.

He didn't move his butt.

"Gee," I tried, commanding him to go right, then, "Haw," for left.

Instead, he eyed the tree with suspicion. He gave it a few sniffs, lifted one hind leg, and took a huge piss on my $200 tree.

I cursed. I probably said, "Jesus, oh my gosh." I tend to say that.

I'm pretty sure local people were looking at me wondering, "Why didn't she just put it in a truck? Or get it delivered?"

I gave up. I unclipped the dog and he took off to chase something, maybe the scent of a rock ptarmigan. I picked up the rope and slowly began to drag the tree home. A wind came off the bay. The force kept pushing me back. I struggled to move forward. I found relief by turning my body away, walking backwards. The tree was heavier than I thought. I yanked at it, stopping every few feet to give my arms a break. It took me a half-hour to go the six blocks to home.

The second we stepped in, Qimmiq curled up like a

cooked shrimp in one corner of the living room. His eyes stared warily at the frozen tree thawing on the other side. It stank so I spritzed some Febreeze. I hoped Frank would be happy that I had bought it.

"You outdid yourself. I was going to surprise you but you beat me to it. Wouldn't be the same without one." Frank grinned and insisted we go back to the Northern Store to get decorations. He had a point. It was a pretty sad, naked, and slightly shredded bit of seasonal shrubbery.

So off we went to get ripped off again, purchasing lights, ornaments, garland, and a topper. Next to the woodstove I hung up the sock matching the one in the doorknob hole. Then, I was ready to flop. I was exhausted, still cold, and looking forward to spending a quiet evening with Frank.

"We're going to be late if we don't get ready for the community feast tonight," Frank reminded me.

I may have muttered, "Jesus, crap. Pass me the rum and Coke."

Admittedly, this was Frank's moment and the reason why I was there, to attend the feast and dance at the John Ollie Hall. But all I wanted to do was crash on the sofa, just like Qimmiq, another cooked shrimp.

What would people say if I didn't show up? My job was to be his accessory, to be someone you saw on TV, recognizable, and then to be seen on his arm. I was an endorsement, a southerner who comes from Yellowknife, with a high-profile job, looking good, being his girlfriend winning more votes. I owed it to him. Frank looked after me. Frank supported me. He treated me better than my father treated my mother. All I need to do was pin a smile on. It was just one lousy evening, wasn't it? After this, the weight would be off. I could let go after I made sure not to let anyone down. Not me, not Frank.

Frank put on jeans and cowboy boots. He didn't bother with a tie but wore a plaid shirt I had bought for him. With his slick sealskin parka on, Frank looked like he was ready to go hunting. It made him fit in. I probably wore something I would wear on television. Something red, something Christmassy. It made me stand out.

The community feast was the social event of the year. The gym was wall-to-wall with constituents feeding off the pent-up energy stored over the first few months of freeze-up. It was sweaty and claustrophobic. Not to Frank. He had on a megawatt smile and oozed charm by the bucketful. With Joey, his constituency assistant, as his translator, Frank worked the gym, making sure he hit all the bigwigs in this town of three thousand. The bounty from hunters lay on tables and upon pieces of cardboard. Racks of caribou, steaming caribou stew, deep purple red seal meat, blush pink muktuk, arctic char, and deep-fried bannock. Folks sat cross-legged on the floor and ate. Others square danced. Bodies shimmied and bounced to the beat of the music. I sat under the exit sign with a plate balanced on my knee and a can of Coke in one hand. An uneaten cube of glistening muktuk vibrated on my plate from the heavy foot stomping and the whine of the fiddle. I had the urge to leave. A piece of stringy caribou stuck in the back of my molars. I got up and went to the washroom to see if I could dig it out. In one stall, someone had scrawled, "I would pee here again," and gave it a two-star rating.

The mirror above the sink was dirty and surrounded by some silver garland. Sad festive. My eyes slid past a recruitment ad to join the Canadian Rangers and protect Arctic sovereignty. Crossed out with a sharpie was the slogan, "BE YOUR BEST!" I flossed, fixed my hair, freshened my lipstick.

On the gym floor, people were throwing themselves into the square dance. They were full of joy, unselfconscious, and I should have joined them. I couldn't dance like them though. It wasn't in me.

Frank sidled up. "It'll be good for them to see us."

I knew to dance here, now. I would have to put my emotion into it. I would have to let loose. But I also knew I would be robotic. I would drag people down if I stepped onto the floor. I understood it was a have-to moment, but my heart wasn't in it. I said, "I'm not working."

He gives me a pleading smile.

I shrugged him off me. "You go on. You don't need me here."

"Suit yourself." His lips narrowed in a thin line, and he headed back onto the floor.

The next day was Christmas Eve. Frank and I made the rounds visiting the elders in the community and drinking cups of tea. He chatted more with the elders than with me. He was still ticked off at me but it didn't bother me. His coolness was mild compared to what my parents dished out to each other.

We went to church that evening, Anglican Midnight Mass. It was crammed with worshippers. There was no heat so I kept my parka on. An Inuit man stood in the sanctuary wearing a long, white garment. I couldn't help staring at his high-top sneakers peeking out from under his robe. He had a big belly and an exquisite, smiling, cherubic face. He had a nice voice. It was soothing. He spoke in Inuktitut. My eyes closed. The sermon started to drift out from the woodgrain speakers of my parent's living room Zenith upon which sat a porcelain Buddha. His mouth kept flapping.

Frank gave me the elbow.

I tried to sit up, but my body slid lower into the wooden pew. I was groggy and I slipped back into peace.

Frank jabbed a few more elbows into my side. I had completely conked out. I brushed away the drool that had dribbled down my chin. Eventually, the sermon wound down and Frank helped me home.

On Christmas Day, we prepared a turkey, lounged around

while it roasted, and finished the rum. Not too long afterward, Frank was snoring on the sofa from turkey coma. I helped myself to more turkey a few hours later. It was lukewarm. Soon, a nagging ache turned into a full-blown roiling pain in my stomach. Then came the waves of nausea. Projectile vomiting reduced me to a sweaty-faced miserable heap on the bathroom floor. I got up two days later, just in time to pack up and fly back to Yellowknife with Frank.

Joey pulled up on his Ski-Doo or ATV and waited at the door. Frank dragged the Rubbermaid to the entrance and handed Turtle to Joey.

I had run out of time to find someone in the community who could use a sewing machine. Joey would know. Maybe I didn't want to know. It was easier to let go at the door.

"What do you call a turtle in Inuktitut?" I asked.

"Teenage Mutant Ninja!"

Whether in English or any other language, Joey could not know what Turtle meant to me. I waved the question off. "Never mind."

In Yellowknife, I went back to reporting on the Snow King and his kingdom of snow castles carved on Yellowknife Bay. With April came spring break-up time. The ice on the castle roofs drooped like soft meringue and then collapsed. The turrets, towers, and bridges dissolved.

I moved to Halifax with Qimmiq. I guess I liked the dog more than Frank.

Our Book of Days

JANE HARRIS

i. During a whiteout, snow blinds us to everything but dark objects

Some people think deer don't belong in the cemetery because they eat the flowers. Not me. I bring roses to draw the mules and white-tails to the place where your body lies.

The deer are the guardians of the dead. They stay to walk among you after the groundskeepers go home—through all seasons, in good weather and bad. They never leave you alone for long, even if we who loved you get too busy to visit.

Only a blizzard can make the deer retreat temporarily from the prairie. I don't know exactly where they go when the arctic wind comes storming over the mountains to whip up snowy whirls. Do you? Is it in the valley, nearer the river? Do they hide with the rabbits and magpies among the cottonwood trees and chokecherry bushes? Do you go with them?

We buried you five days before Christmas, in the middle of a blizzard when the polar vortex pushed thermometers to -40°C. It was not yet four in the afternoon when we got to your grave, but it felt like dusk. It was supposed to be the second darkest day of the year. I think it was the darkest.

I didn't see any deer the day we buried you. If they came, they kept their distance. But then again, I couldn't see much of anything through the blizzard. Your sister and brother kept me from falling while we waded to the chair in front of your grave. I did glimpse the oak-stained wooden urn your father and I picked out for you, and your picture propped on the bench beside it. That picture was taken in a sunny mountain valley on a day when your smile lit up our world. But the afternoon we buried you, there was no sun. It was so cold that the flower arrangements we ordered for your service froze the minute they were taken out of the hearse. White flakes landed on the wreath of yellow mums we brought from the funeral home, and the cold flash-froze the white roses piled in a heap beside you.

I sat. Everyone else stood. Your sister clasped her icy hands around my neck. She'd forgotten to bring her mitts. I wrapped my gloved fingers around her bare skin. "Let me warm you up," I said. As if anything could keep away the cold that afternoon.

The priest prayed for you—ashes to ashes and dust to dust. The funeral director wrapped your urn in a purple velvet pouch before he placed it in the earth. I was comforted by that. I didn't want you to be cold.

Somebody handed me a rose to toss on your coffin. I

stood up and pointed the long stem toward you. It landed crossways and got stuck near the opening. Your sister's husband leaned over to push it into the pit. Your father tossed his rose, then your sister and your brother tossed theirs. They aimed better.

I wondered why the city crew made the hole so deep. I wondered why I hadn't put my hand on the urn when your father and I lit your baptismal candle in the funeral home. Why had I waited until now to think of touching you again? Why didn't I turn the camera on for our last Facebook chat? It was too late.

I wanted to hold my baby again.

The funeral director said the deer would eat the yellow flowers if we left them on the grave. I thought that was fine, but no one else did. I wanted to take some home, but your dad and brother said it wasn't a good idea because they were frozen. Your father said to bury all the flowers with you. So that's what we did.

I imagined your spirit standing a few feet back, laughing at us all for talking about what to do with flowers in the middle of a blizzard. I imagined you standing among the deer waving goodbye to us. I thought how beautiful this white garden was—like Narnia in winter.

The deer didn't get their supper, but we did. We went to your father's house where your stepmother laid out your favourite cold cuts on the dining room table beside overflowing vegetable, fruit, and dessert trays. She bustled around her kitchen making coffee and tea—trying to get everything right when nothing could be right. I sat in the living room like a block of ice, catching snippets of conversations floating around me. My flesh and blood were ashes and dust.

Your brother and his fiancée drove me back to my apartment. It took us nearly an hour to cross the ice-covered bridge in the storm. I was home by seven. It felt like midnight.

Your funeral was Tuesday. On Wednesday, it was too cold to go outside, so I ordered presents on Amazon, knowing some wouldn't arrive until Boxing Day. On Thursday, I wrapped myself in my black fur coat, hat, mitts, scarf, and boots. I stuffed shopping bags in my purse. I dug my walking stick into the ice and crossed the road to the bus stop.

Gasping for air and hanging on to the rail to stop the wind from throwing me into traffic, I watched the blasts spin twigs and wrappers along the street. I could have hidden my grief from store clerks, but these gusts brought me to tears. So, I went home. I ordered groceries and candles to be delivered on Friday night.

It warmed a bit by Sunday, Christmas Day. At dinner, we remembered you and we toasted spring.

*

ii. Christmastide is when babies save the world

Who put the Christmas wreath on your grave? Who trudged through six inches of snow in coldest December to get to you? It was not your father, your sister, or your brother. Not your grandparents, your aunts, or your uncle. It was not me.

I found the twisted pine boughs tied to your marker when I brought white roses for you and the deer in January. And there they stayed, fading to deep khaki, then earthy brown, until the city crews cleared away rubbish and mowed lawns just before Holy Week. They were expecting visitors. The cemetery is a busy place in the summer. You know that already, don't you?

Do you remember when we used to hike behind the cemetery on our way to the river valley when you were a little boy? We were happy on those Sunday afternoons. Do you remember how you, your dad, brother, sister, and I delighted in foraging for wild chokecherries and Saskatoon berries on our walks? Remember how we dipped our hands into the cold water when we finally made it to the river shore? In those days we must have looked like a perfect family to the hikers we passed on our way down to the water. We weren't, of course. You already knew that.

Still, on those magical Sundays we never thought much about the people in the graves as we passed by the cemetery on our hikes. Your dad and I never dreamed that we would have to visit you there someday. Our world had not yet fallen apart. Though we were already on the edge of disaster, we didn't know it yet. We were luckier than we knew.

After you died, we picked Mountain View cemetery as your resting place, partly because the mountains you loved are visible on a clear day and partly because it's in the centre of town, close to the house you lived in when you were little. We wanted to bring you to a place where you were happy, and you were happiest in that southside neighbourhood that's knitted together by the greenstrips where you once rode your bike, went tobogganing, and hiked.

I never realized how truly busy the inside pathways of the cemetery were, though, until your stepfather died five years ago. That's when I first moved from passing by on my way to other places and became a regular visitor inside its gates. That's when I discovered that the graveyard is filled with living hikers and bikers and dog walkers. Its paved and shaded pathways are a favourite haunt of joggers in the spring and summer. Indeed sometimes these recreational users outnumber the mourners.

Still, it's mostly relatives of the dead who visit at Christmas. When the weather's good in December, they bring tinsel and greenery to the cemetery. This discovery amazed me the first winter after your stepfather died, when I came with a bouquet in late December and noticed green wreaths, frozen flower petals, and half-eaten foliage—remains of the deer's holiday feast—dotting the snow.

Since then, I've noticed that one family usually leaves a six-foot Christmas tree with tinsel and ornaments on a grave in the block across the road from you, near where your stepfather is buried. Not this year, though. It took a determined soul to put that wreath on your grave in the middle of the arctic freeze; someone who knows that Christmas is a blazing fire of relentless hope in the dead of winter; someone who defies darkness, affirms light, and knows that spring must return and that evil cannot win forever and that love is stronger than death. It took someone who loved you, too. That made me smile and I wanted to cry, too, because you didn't always feel love after you got sick, but for me you were the very definition of love.

It was always December when I found out I was pregnant. The first time I was twenty-one and wearing a wedding ring. But I looked eighteen and I was nervous. So, maybe that's why the nurse asked me if I was sure I wanted to have a baby when she gave me the test result. I stared at her in disbelief. Couldn't she see that you were the best Christmas present ever?

It is true that your father sat by the stereo and played Neil Young's "Got Mashed Potatoes" over and over again before I left to go to the doctor. But we knew we'd be able to feed you and keep you warm. We knew we were not alone.

When you were born, your dad's mother helped us buy a house with blackberry bushes in the flower beds, a plum tree in the garden, and peach saplings beside the fence. On your first Christmas and every Christmas after that, she arrived with suitcases full of presents, cookies, and fruitcakes. You called her "Knittin" instead of "Grandma" because she spent her afternoons making blankets, sweaters, and mittens for you.

When you were seventeen months old, I snapped a picture of you, rosy-cheeked and beaming, running towards me hugging a battery-operated Santa you found in Knittin's suitcase. You had sunlight in your hair and eyes, joy spread across your face. I kept that picture by my bed all the years that you were sick.

iii. Lent can last a decade

It was 2013. You came home for Christmas, clearly not well, too skinny for your tall frame. Fresh from a breakup with your live-in girlfriend. You drank too much at dinner— something I had never seen you do before. I told the other kids I was worried. They said you would be fine now that you were home.

You stayed at your father's house for six months, but I didn't see you much. It wasn't unusual for you not to call when you were with your dad. I knew the reasons why. So, I didn't worry.

I didn't hear about the conspiracies circulating in your mind until that Saturday morning in June when you texted me from Toronto. You talked about Nazis and stolen inheritances. You said you wanted to hurt people. Nobody but me knew that you were gone.

We soon learned that's how it was when you got sick. You disappeared without a trace. Went silent for weeks. I tried to find you when I won a trip to Toronto for a writer's conference, but you didn't want to be found until you lost your job and had no place to live. You begged for help then. So did I.

I spent hours on the phone trying to get support for you when you were homeless, confused, and afraid in that metropolis. A Toronto cop told me that there were too many poor to help, that we had to leave them on the street. I told him he should quit his job because he had no heart before I hung up on him. I convinced a street ministry to help you,but you didn't like what they were preaching.

A few days later, your old girlfriend sent you money for a Greyhound ride back to BC. She still loved you. But you were sicker than she thought. Not sick enough for the doctors to keep you in the psychiatric ward for thirty days, though. That Christmas, you wound up alone, living in a hotel on social assistance, not getting better.

After you died, the front-desk clerk said you kept to

yourself, that you liked climbing mountain trails and swimming at the outdoor pool. When your things came home, I found your poetry in the old books you collected. Your handwriting was beautiful, even, and clear. Some of the words didn't make sense, but even when you were ill, there could be wisdom in your words.

We waited for a miracle for seven years.

You wouldn't talk to your father, and sometimes you didn't answer me, but I sent birthday and Christmas presents. Sometimes you'd thank me. Sometimes you'd say you loved me. Sometimes you weren't in the mood for talking, so I'd check in with the staff at the place you lived to make sure you were okay. They liked you. You always paid your rent on time, were polite, and you never made a ruckus. No one could believe you overdosed and died in your room.

The last Christmas you were alive, the courier didn't deliver your presents, and you didn't go to pick them up. So, I mailed you a gift card for your birthday. It got there late. But you were ready to talk to me again.

I told you I was sorry because the Christmas gifts never arrived and I hadn't mailed your birthday present on time. I told you that I was late with everything these days, that I couldn't walk without sticks, and the doctor didn't know why. I sent you a photo of my grey cat—because you loved grey cats. That made you happy for a moment or two.

Then you told me that you were getting older day by day

and that you felt like you had run out of time. I told you it wasn't true. That you were young enough to start again. I let you know that I loved you.

I still believed we would get you help and bring you home again. I didn't understand that you were saying goodbye.

I watched the first passion-pink bloom open on my gnarled Christmas cactus on November 18th—a week and day after the coroner said you died. It rarely blooms anymore. But last year cascading flowers spilled out and pointed themselves toward the sunlight until mid-February.

I was almost ready for Christmas by the time the police came. I'd cleaned the house, put up the tree, and thought of what to buy you. I'd polished your silver baby cup and moved your Santa picture to the foyer—tamping down the fear that woke me up every night. Sure, you'd been silent before, but this time it felt like you had left the world.

On Thursday—the night they found you—I slept long and deep. I didn't wake up until after noon on Friday. I decided to bake bread. As I placed the last loaves in the oven, the bell rang. I don't usually open the door unless I know who's there, but on the 25th of November I buzzed the visitors in and ran to the lobby. The tallest cop I ever saw and two women from Victims' Services insisted on coming in. It was about 5:00 pm.

iv. We danced your song on the last day of Easter

We left an empty seat for you in the front row at your brother's wedding in May. Did you come? Did you see the stag that stepped out of nowhere to stare into the window while we waited for the bride?

He was a mule deer, the black tuft on his tail gave him away, taller than any I had ever seen before, with newly sprung velvet-covered antlers, charcoal grey. They had grown enough to make his giant ears look like they fit his head. I was transfixed by the ruddiness of his coat and the strength of his chest. Perhaps it was the greenness of the baby grass and emerging leaves behind him that made him look redder than most deer around here. The buck's haughty gaze told us he wanted nothing from us, unlike the shivering does who come meekly, begging shelter on my patio in winter.

I wondered if his antlers would get as big as the rack I found in my grandmother's attic when I was a little girl. Did I ever tell you about those antlers? They were from a stag my Swedish great-grandfather shot when he first came to this country. My brother has them now. Old Anders, so the family legend goes, was a wanderer—mad, addicted, or maybe both. A dreamer whose adventures never turned out right. He died alone, too.

The stag had returned to the valley by the time your brother and the sister-in-law you will never meet began their married life dancing to Randy Travis' "Forever and Ever, Amen." We didn't see the deer leave.

A few days later, the girl you brought to my second wedding emailed me to say that you used to sing that song over and over again to Wilson the cat when you lived with her. She said hearing it gave her chills. She said you would have loved to hear that song again. Were you in the room with us when they played it?

Eastertide and the wedding both ended at midnight. The next morning, Pentecost Sunday, I brought you and the deer a bouquet of bright yellow lilies. My parents and your aunt came, too. They took pictures of your grave and left an angel beside your marker. Then we returned to Ordinary Time without you.

Though I have been to the place you're buried a dozen times, my mind still can't grasp that you are dead. I want to undo time and bring you back. I want to release you from the trap. I want to find a way to make you well. I want to make you live again. I want a miracle that my faith says cannot happen until the end of time. But tiny miracles are everywhere, if you look for them: the sweet ripe apples that fall on to my path in September, a poem that writes itself at 4:00 am, the sound of your voice inside my head, and the deer that seem to seek me out.

I saw a fawn in June, a few weeks after your brother's wedding. It was the day after the summer solstice—the tenth anniversary of the unravelling of our lives—the second lightest day of the year. The newborn was nestled in the grass, waiting patiently for his mother, knowing she would return for him because that's what mothers are supposed to do. Mothers are a little like God in that way. Anyway, when I saw the fawn, I knew what I needed to say to you. It's this: I will miss you forever, but I carry your memory everywhere. I will never leave you behind, but I am going to be okay. Your brother and sister will be, too. So will you, until we meet again. I love you always and forever, amen. Love, Mum.

P.S.

Another year has passed. I still wish I could undo time and bring you back to me. I still think about you every day, but I have amazing news. Maybe you know it already. You are going to be an uncle, and the deer have started seeking out your brother. In mid-June—the week of the summer solstice—newborn twin fawns and their mother joined him on one of the walks he takes at lunch. The next day, he and his wife got their first ultrasound, the one that confirmed that they are expecting twins sometime in late December. The twin fawns met him again in early July, much bigger and on their own this time, while their mother was feeding on the greenstrip. A week later, on your birthday, the second ultrasound confirmed the human babies are strong, too, and growing quickly as the fawns. They will be here at Christmas, and we are happy again.

Somehow, I think you do know this already. I think maybe that's what the deer and you have been trying to tell me for the past year and half: that after the mourning, comes new life. And babies still save the world at Christmas.

Missing and loving you always, Mum.

Songbird

JILL MAYNARD

I sat at our dining room table, hot cup of tea in hand, with one eye on four suitcases sitting in a row at the front door and another eye looking outside the window where there was a stillness that can only be found in those early pre-dawn hours.

The streetlights cast a soft, golden glow that shimmered on slick pavement and Christmas lights, wrapped around cedar trunks sparkling through a light drizzle. It was soothing.

Inside was anything but soothing. Rowan, age eleven, was in full "skipper" mode. Always my right-hand man, he moved the suitcases out to the van, letting in a cold blast of air each time he entered or left the house.

Two-year-old Niklas, wanting to emulate his older brother, appointed himself the master of snacks. I heard the fridge close and he toddled out of the kitchen with a huge jar of dill pickles, the same width as his head, slipping through the grip of his tiny hands.

He loved pickles, had gotten them from Santa, and wanted, it seemed, to pack them, and maybe nibble on a few. Who wants to have a pickle at four o'clock in the morning?

"Ohhh, Niklas, no."

I reached for the jar before it dropped and became a flood of stench and broken glass. "We can't bring pickles on the plane. How about you throw the ball for the dog outside?"

Niklas adapted the plan by playing fetch with Joe Blue inside. Not perfect, but at least they were both distracted.

Marly, at nine, was always filling our house with chatter and she liked to narrate her life with melodious singing. At this moment, her eyes fluttered as she reached the high notes. "We're going to Maui in the middle of the night, and the world is still asleep."

Rowan helping, Niklas being Niklas, my little songbird chattering. It was predictable bustle, true to their nature, the music of my life as a mother. I was happy.

Marly stopped singing. "None of my friends could possibly be awake at this hour, right, Momma?"

"Of course, they're all asleep," I replied. But I understood her. It was a novelty for Marly to be awake when everybody else she knew remained asleep. This was special. It really was. We were heading to Maui with my parents on an extended post-Christmas vacation.

Some of my favourite childhood memories were of the island: the feel of the warm breeze, the scent of plumeria, crossing a gravel road to the Whalers Village strip mall to get passion fruit shaved ice. But this trip would be different. My mom was deep into a diagnosis of Alzheimer's.

I was hoping somehow that we could still hold on, that

we could still handle this. We could do a family vacation with my parents to Maui. And it could be as idyllic as it was when I was a child.

My husband couldn't come with us. He couldn't miss work or overcome his fear of flying. I was okay with it. In the end, it would be easier to have fewer moving parts, people wanting to do different things, people having different needs to accommodate. Caring for Mom was no small undertaking, even at home, and it already had taken a toll on Dad. Her illness threatened to erode his *joie de vivre*.

I sat quietly for another minute at the dining room table, allowing the chaos in the house to become background noise. I continued looking out the window. My attention was drawn to the lights lining the asymmetrical roofline of my neighbour's house. One bulb blinked, erratic, in the otherwise solid string. I can not suffer blinking lights. My whole family knows it.

In fact, my family—all jokers—used to plant a blinking tungsten or LED anywhere, anytime like Halloween, and put it on the most frenetic setting possible to test how long it would be before I lost my shit and removed it. Yes, lights going on and off make me, let's say, tense.

I fantasized about ninja'ing over and unscrewing the light so I didn't have to watch it blink. It was 4:00 am. Who would notice?

Rowan finished loading the van and jumped in triumph.

He stretched his lithe arms and reached up for the back hatch, his fingers hardly getting purchase on its icy edge. On tiptoes, he did manage to pull the door down and slam it. He clapped his hands and propelled himself up the stairs and into the house. "It's time to go pick up Grammy and Grampy! I can't believe we get to go somewhere hot in the winter, Mom!"

The family loaded in and my husband, playing chauffeur, pulled out of the driveway onto deserted streets and we left the wonky light behind. The kids and I were off on a tropical winter vacation.

My parents stood waiting in a faint beam of light at the top of their driveway, suitcases at their feet. "Who do we have here?" Dad peered inside the van. "Where is Niklas? I thought he was coming too?"

"Bapa! I'm right here!" Niklas called out.

"Oh, there you are. I am so glad you decided to come. Can I sit beside you?"

Niklas giggled as Dad climbed into the back seat. Mom laughed too, only she didn't know why. But, hearing my Dad's jovial banter reassured me. I still had a parent.

My husband pulled up to the departures terminal and unloaded our suitcases onto the curb. Rowan held Niklas while I wrestled the stroller out. Dad held Mom's hand and Marly bounced around us all, looking up at my husband. She pleaded, "Daddy, are you *suuure* you can't come?"

Marly tilted her head to the side. She was literally hopping around us. Good. She was excited. She never liked the family being separated and clearly, even at this last moment, held out hope that my husband might come after all.

"No, Sweetie, but you will have a great time. Find some turtles for me!"

As we said our goodbyes and waved through the closing airport doors, I worried about how Mom would handle navigating check-in, security, and flying.

Alzheimer's decline is not a gradual slope. Abilities fall away like they were pushed over a cliff. One day she could get dressed. The next she could not. Rowan remembered a grandmother who could pick him up from daycare and take him on outings. Marly was once able to do art projects with her and play games in the yard. Niklas only knew my real Mom from videos. "Grammy could talk?" he asked.

They didn't know that this would be our last trip with my mom before Alzheimer's took all of her. Dad didn't want to talk about it on this trip and neither did I. I was determined to tuck my anxiety away and put on a brave face.

On the plane, we sat in two rows. Marly, my mom, and my dad in front of Rowan, Niklas, and me. Marly had the window seat and hummed as usual. She was rapt by the view. She leaned into the pane. Dawning sunlight fell on her face. "Mom, I have never seen clouds from above before."

I watched through the gap between the windows and the seat: the light beams in her hair, the look of peace and innocence on her face. I heard her sing, revealing so much of herself and how she sees the world, in a string of notes. Nothing is held inside. She sang, "A cloud inside out."

I was aglow.

Marly stopped. My mom for no reason unbuckled and tried to get up. We directed her to sit back. She grew frustrated. Dad and I glanced at each other. I wondered if we'd made a mistake.

The boys started playing a game. Marly popped up and looked over the back of her seat to see what was going on. I thought I'd tell them about Maui and the times I had spent there as a child.

Kihei was always the Maynard go-to. "It's drier on that side!" my grandpa always said. My grandparents, great aunt and uncle, and other extensions of my dad's family all converged on the beaches of Kamaole, taking up several suites at the Royal Mauian. I told the kids about being free, walking wherever I wanted because there was so much family around. My little brother and I would play shuffleboard, swim for hours, and perform theatrical skits for any family willing to watch. Our finest work was known as the "Wounded Swan Dance."

I would jump up and down in the outdoor pool executing different ballet moves as I burst through the surface of the water. Always with a nose plug and an expressive look on my face as if I were singing an opera.

I told them about the colourful muumuus, the creation of the Maynard family signature beverage (rum and ginger ale), and all the Maynards watching the sunset to confirm the existence of the green flash, the mythical last light of day. That Maui felt safe and unchangeable. I looked at it then with a sense of permanence.

Out of nowhere, Marly asked, "Are there poisonous things in Maui?"

I had a sudden need to avert her anxiousness. There had been hints of her anxiety, but I hadn't pieced together how significant it was. My own anxieties had always been around. The sound of fans, inexplicable fear of family members coming to harm, and those blinking lights. But I was trying not to inflict what I had on Marly. I didn't want to pass it to her. I tried to divert her back to more positive images.

"No, actually. They don't have any poisonous bugs or snakes," I assured her. "But, we have seen turtles right on the beach where we will be staying."

I was trying to keep the focus on the good stuff. I rambled. "As soon as you step off the plane you will notice the air. It smells tropical and is warm and a bit muggy."

Niklas looked at me. "Like cups?"

"Ha! No, it's like the air is hot and it makes you feel a bit sweaty."

✳

"I don't like sweaty!" Niklas wrinkled his nose up.

"Well, actually there is usually quite a nice breeze."

"Mom," Niklas interrupted. "Mom, we're sleeping at Maui?"

"Yes," I say. I wanted to add that I hope he sleeps a lot, but I stopped myself.

"What about jellyfish and sharks?" It was Marly. "Can I just swim in the pool?"

"There are lots of great places to swim and we can stay close to shore. But you know what I love the most?"

They all look at me.

"The birds," I said. "It's the fact that their songs sound different from where we live. You'll notice that. Like a different soundtrack to life."

"Can we go to the pool as soon as we get there?" Marly asks.

The coastline came into view and I was relieved.

We heard the announcement. "We are starting our descent into Maui. The local time is 2:53 pm and the temperature is thirty-six degrees. Flight attendants, please prepare for landing."

Marly hummed as the plane descended. Peace was restored.

Maui inhabits you before your feet even hit the ground. Sweet, humid air telling you everything is going to be okay.

At our hotel in Kihei, Christmas lingered in the lobby. Carols were still playing and the decorations looked tired. We were on the sixth floor and our apartment looked over a grove of palm trees set between a carpet of perfect lawn and a fine sand beach.

On the first morning, I awoke to the unearthly sound of Marly talking to me through a snorkel, a Vader-esque inhale followed by her saying, "We are ready for the pool!"

Her flippers slapped the tile floor. She was one hundred percent pool-ready. It was sunrise. Thankfully, the pool was still closed. I had time that morning to sit on the lanai with a cup of tea in my hands. I watched the palms wave, the water glisten turquoise, and listened to a chorus of tropical birds.

By 8:00 am the kids and I were heading to the pool, only to be turned around by a blue-haired octogenarian who pointed to a sign on the pool gate. It was seniors only until nine every morning. The only option was the beach. Marly relented and ran there with Rowan. Niklas and I followed.

By the time we had caught up, Rowan and Marly were running up from the surf, wet and salty. They rolled in the sand, then raced back to the water's edge.

Niklas sat beside me, his blue shovel deep into a growing hole. All our inhibitions were lost to the joys of heat, sand, and sun. A small sandy foot brushed my leg. I turned to look at Niklas.

"Niklas, what are you doing?"

"I'm eating sand."

"Why? Why are you eating sand?"

"I really love it."

"You love eating sand?"

"Yeah. You have some?" He held up a sandy finger for me to lick.

"I think I am okay, buddy."

I wiggled my feet into the sand. That was when I heard it. A sound was coming from my phone, one I had never heard before. It made the hairs on my arm stand up. I pulled out my phone. Words flashed on the screen. All in capital letters. They didn't enter my brain the way capital letters should, sturdy and resolute. They shattered and shook like an earthquake.

EMERGENCY ALERT.

BALLISTIC MISSILE THREAT INBOUND TO HAWAII.

SEEK IMMEDIATE SHELTER.

THIS IS NOT A DRILL.

I saw others looking at their phones, turning to each other, picking up their stuff, heading off the beach.

"Hey kids, we have to go check in with Grammy and Grampy for a bit."

I avoided their bewilderment.

"But we just got out here?"

I am not even sure which one of them asked. "Just do what I need you to do, right now."

We followed a stream of people into the hotel. As soon as we entered the building, my intention to muster with my parents and keep the kids in the dark collapsed.

Staff standing in the lobby shepherded everybody toward the stairs. "Please follow the group into the basement gym where we will wait."

I will always wonder why I followed that instruction. I could have broken away from the group, returned to our room, and found my parents. But I followed the directions and the option to withhold the truth shrank. I didn't have a reference point for how to handle this. How do you hide from a missile?

Help them be safe and help them feel safe. Both things seemed critical and I didnt know how to do either. I didn't want them to feel panic and fear, so that is what I focused on. I could help them feel safe, maybe.

The basement smelled of stale sweat and rubber. We were tucked into a nook between a treadmill and a leg press.

"Mom, why are we down here?" Rowan asked. "Was there a drunk guy on the beach?"

He made me want to laugh but I didn't because there was a possibility we were about to die.

"It's a little more than that, Rowan."

I looked at a woman standing next to me. She was in her

late fifties. She wore a soft blue dress with an uneven hem over her bathing suit and layered beaded bracelets on her right arm. She wasn't as old as my mom, but her proximity soothed me.

A man from the hotel appeared in the doorway, his hands pressed against the frame as he leaned in slightly. He had the energy of somebody in charge but not quite to the level required for ballistic ordnance. "The cell reception is okay down here, but it's better in the hallway. If you want to make some goodbye calls."

My jaw dropped. What the fuck? I had kids.

He laughed nervously and disappeared.

A man behind us phoned home. "You saw my message? I need to tell you where I put the dog licence."

Marly tugged on my skirt. "Mom. What's a goodbye call?"

A clear voice emerged—a woman on vacation from Oahu who claimed, loudly, connections to the Marine Corps. She commanded attention by demanding it of everyone in the room.

She dialled with a flourish, her arms extended out. "Hello, sir. Can I get an update, sir?" I imagined her heels clicking together in heavy boots in rhythm to each syllable as she spoke, but in reality she wore a tight tank-top, Lululemon shorts, and cute pink runners. I wondered where she got them.

The man behind us ended his call. I didn't hear where the dog licence was. Another man shrugged his shoulders, chortled, and said, "Well, I'm opting for burial at sea."

He walked out of the room, a towel slung over his shoulder.

"Mom," Marly tugged again on my sundress, "what is a goodbye call?"

"Momma, look at me!" Niklas now swung from the arm of the treadmill.

I wanted to get out of the basement to protect them from words. I needed to stay in the basement to protect them from the missile. I looked at my shivering kids covered with sand. I felt completely inadequate. I can't even keep my kids warm in the tropics.

"Thank you, sir." Marine Corps Lady hung up. "A missile has been launched. America has responded." The kids heard her. Marly heard her, one hundred percent. Her words were their own missile.

I texted Dad. No response.

A question was asked, "How long do we have until it lands?"

Marine Corp Lady answered, "About twenty minutes."

It would take twelve more minutes before the fragility of life had sunk in for two of my kids. Niklas, however, was oblivious. He swung boldly on the gym equipment. As long as he was next to me, he felt safe. I could do that for him.

*

Dad sent a text. They were walking on the beach. They had the beach entirely to themselves. Dad was sure it was some kind of mistake. Was he doing for me the same thing I was doing for the kids?

I received a message from my boss. "Buddy, please, tell me you are okay."

Eight minutes before the estimated time of impact, worry crossed Rowan's face. "Where is the missile going to land?"

I steadied my voice. "They won't aim at Keawapaku Beach. They will target a major city centre."

It was a grim offering.

Marly's blue eyes looked up at me, wet blond hair glued to her face. "Are we going to die?"

She gripped her wet snorkel in her hand, water still dripping onto the floor.

At six minutes, I knew I had to answer. "I don't think so, my sweet."

I looked out a small window. I could see the tops of palm trees. They swayed in a soft breeze. The morning sun flickered through the branches. This natural blinking light didn't bother me at all. It was strangely comforting.

Marine Corps Lady received a call. The room went quiet. Her words would be our fate. Some deep instinctual part of me wanted to influence those words. As if their content was of our choosing. She hung up the phone.

"False alarm."

I exhaled and realized I may have been holding my breath the whole time. I laughed in an unhinged way. It was not a true laugh. It didn't quite belong to me. It was a cry in disguise.

Released from our basement tomb, we returned to the warmth of the sun. My legs shook. I wiggled my feet into the grass of the lawn, planting myself into the living earth.

Rowan and Marly gripped my hands. Niklas, joyfully clueless, collected sticks.

It was 9:30 in the morning. I found my mom and dad, and I took them all to Whalers Village, to the shaved-ice shack.

Dad and I ordered iced lattes; I needed some caffeine. We got a shaved ice for Mom, but I didn't pay attention to the flavour. The kids had mango, guava, and lime.

Mom took a heaping spoonful to her lips, smiled at the flood of sweetness, then grimaced in pain—brain freeze. She had the bliss of a child, with no idea of what had happened that morning. All my worries about my mom had been displaced.

I watched my daughter. Her head was down. She leaned so that her shoulder touched Rowan's. She held her shaved ice in one hand, the spoon in the other. Her arms rested on her knees. Her shave-ice melted under the sun, iridescent rivers of colour dripping down her hands onto the ground.

My little songbird was silent.

*

The missile would never land, except on Marly. In nine months time, I would drive white-knuckled with a tearful Marly to an anxiety support group. When the kids were asked to write down what made them feel anxious, most wrote "piano recitals," "sports," and "public speaking." Marly wrote "ballistic missiles."

2 South

LÉA TARANTO

The Stewart and Lynda Resnick Neuropsychiatric Hospital at UCLA was an eleven-storey, terracotta brick behemoth of a building. It had a central spine with wings housing separate psych units for different age groups and eating disorders. There were common areas like the green asphalt soccer field for outdoor recreation, the glass-enclosed rooftop with lawn bowling and basketball hoops, the giant occupational therapy workshop, cafeteria, school room, and even a gift shop.

While I had done a stint on 2 West, the eating disorders ward, I ended up living on 2 South, the child and adolescent psych ward, since my obsessive-compulsive disorder had upstaged my anorexia.

Back then my compulsions were still weight-loss focused, but my obsessions were mutating, fuelled by a childhood of church with my maternal grandma, Poh Poh, and four months at a Christian eating disorders facility, Remuda Ranch. At Remuda, my physical body was saved by tube feeding, while a similar gavage of Bible studies and books like Dante Alighieri's *Inferno* convinced me my eternal soul was damned. Obsessive visions of *Inferno's* worst sinners held me hostage. I was certain that I was among them, having murdered my father in a previous life. In this current life, I loved my mother more than anyone. Therefore, God would harm her to punish me unless I punished myself enough first.

By the time I got to UCLA, Mom would lose a year of her life for every door around me that I didn't personally open and shut; she would feel great pain if I didn't stretch before going to the bathroom; likewise if I didn't punish myself with jumping and stretching for dropping things. She would be severely injured if I didn't do one hundred double leg butt kick jumps before bed and—worst of all— would die if I didn't perform at least three hours of jumping jacks perfectly every morning.

I did the jumping jacks in my room on 2 South because that was the only place I had privacy. Laden with heavy books and a full water bottle that I used as weights, I pushed myself to exhaustion. Screw-ups like miscounting reps, stopping, slowing down, stumbling, touching the walls or furniture, or dropping any of the "weights" meant I had to start from scratch lest God smite Mom.

I had arrived during the summer but now I was in the darkened, somewhat rainy LA winter. By mid-December, I had two blisters on both my big toes. One of them had hardened to a yellow callous with stretched-out skin. The other was much larger and burgundy, full of blood. When I walked, I hobbled in agony. Performing my exercises was worse.

My one hundred nightly butt kick jumps required that

✳

I slam my entire weight down hard on the balls of my feet. Each landing sent jolts of pain through the nerves beneath the blisters. The three hours of morning jumping jacks were much easier on my toes, the pain more a steady, rhythmic twinge as I hyper-focused on counting reps. It lessened after a few hours and became ignorable during afternoons when I sat on my ass for occupational therapy. Yet it never fully disappeared from my awareness until I fell asleep.

When I did lose consciousness, part of me always hoped it would be forever. Then Mom would be safe and I would be free. To die while sleeping wasn't a sin. No one could accuse me of forsaking my life or my loved ones if I wasn't even awake for it.

On 2 West, my religious exercise rituals scared people, so they avoided me. Staff thought I was a lost cause, and my days were a lonely blur of feeling abandoned. Before it could break, I hardened my heart. I learned to keep the pain of others' coldness at bay by setting fire to it as anger. Rage kept me active and alert and gave me energy for my rituals.

But on 2 South, people who were used to patients with strange behaviours would engage with me. Some for good, some for bad. Although none quite as bad as Justine, a tween with developmental disabilities, Tourette's, and the capriciousness of a Greek god. For the two months that she'd been around in early autumn, she'd held a deity-like power over me.

*

In a good mood, Justine was earnestly affectionate. Prone to declaring you her bestest friend and drawing you stick figure cartoons. In a bad mood, Justine was vicious. Prone to violence and willing to use anything at her disposal to make you feel as bad as she did.

When we first met, I'd given her the same spiel I gave everyone, staff or patient, who seemed like a potential friend: a brief explanation of who I was, why I was in treatment, and a plaintive request to please not say a certain common word. Let's use the word "r-i-g-h-t" for this story. While "right" and I are alright (haha) now, reading it back then reduced me to tears. Hearing it was even worse. Anxiety and rage would erupt from me and flow toward whoever had said it unless they convinced me it was accidental.

Justine often threatened to say the r-word unless I played with her. Dolls. Ping Pong. Go Fish, which I always let her win. Justine would say it on purpose. Repeatedly. If upset, she'd scream r-i-g-h-t over and over at me until I fled or flailed. She thought it was funny. The private sanctity of my room meant nothing to her. I would have to hide in the bathroom pretending to crap before she would leave me alone. Fucked up or not, our coercive hot/cold relationship was all either of us had. So, yes, until she was discharged from the unit, I was her bestest friend. After she left, my "indigestion" disappeared. The toilet was no longer my only escape. My room became a refuge instead of a small space

I could be cornered in. I savoured every new card game I learned that wasn't Go Fish. When new kids arrived, I vetted them carefully before giving them the Please-Don't-Say-R-I-G-H-T speech. And I made sure no one else knew that a second word had started bothering me: better.

Better was what everyone wanted from me. Mom begged me to be better. Poh Poh prayed for me to get better. My stepdad, Peter, urged me to do better. Psychiatrists prescribed me ever-changing pill combos to heal better. Mental Health Technicians bribed me with better. The better I behaved, the better my privileges would be. As for me, I knew I could hate me into betterment if only I hated harder.

Four days after Justine left, Lupe arrived, a seventeen-year-old who might have had depression but did a great job hiding it. She was Justine's polar opposite, a calm, caring big sister. She spent most of her free time connecting with other patients or staff. I often saw her chatting up folks in the eating or living room area where tables for poker, ping pong, and a wall-mounted TV with couches were set up. Then there was fourteen-year-old Angel, admitted to 2 South for PTSD. She was a hardcore introvert. But when I wasn't occupied by rituals and Angel felt like socializing, we'd find Lupe and the three of us would watch movies or play Texas Hold'em. They quickly became my closest friends.

The week before Christmas, Lupe was getting discharged.

*

That morning Angel and I woke up early to make our big sis a goodbye card. We ate lunch together for the very last time with the homemade card resting on her bejewelled Juicy duffel bag beneath the table. I couldn't help complaining about how both of them would be home for the holidays, since Angel had been approved for a four-day pass. She'd leave on Christmas Eve and sleep in her actual house for three nights before returning on the 27th.

"Your parents are coming, that's like, the next best thing." Lupe's sparkly silver nails poked my arm. "Keep following the rules and you might even get an overnight pass."

Following the rules . . . As in eating all the cottage cheese from my fruit plate lunch and not hiding several spoonfuls of it in my empty skim milk carton. While the two of them planned a Boxing Day meetup in Santa Monica, I smeared the last of it against the underside of my plate. From above, the smushed white curds were undetectable. Good. Meals on 2 South weren't monitored by staff the way they had been on 2 West, but I still had to finish within thirty minutes and present a clean plate to the nurses. If I did, I could see Mom and Peter when they came on Friday the 23rd. They'd be able to take me on daily afternoon passes and I'd get to eat lunch with them. For one whole week of afternoons we could pretend to be a normal family doing normal touristy things in LA.

Half an hour after Lupe left, I mixed glazes at occupational therapy, a euphemism for arts and crafts time. The giant workshop had plenty of supplies and equipment. Besides canvases and easels for painting, there were pottery wheels and kilns for ceramics, and a sink area with scented oils for candle or soap making. I had already made Mom a pink rose-scented soap and Poh Poh a purple lavender one. Peter's gift was more ambitious, a clay plate. Since he was Dutch and loved all things Holland, I decorated it with a windmill.

The plate was my olive branch to him. Peter valued intelligence, logic, and dignity, things that I had long since replaced with dieting facts and controlling rituals. During my last year at home, my disorders demanded things of not only me, but everyone around me. I became fiercely competitive and protective of any kind of action that could be construed as exercise, everything from washing dishes and vacuuming to lifting heavy objects like groceries, crockery, and even the flat-screen TV that Peter had bought with a raise. Why couldn't he let me carry the new TV from the car to the living room? Did he think I would drop it? Did he think I wasn't strong enough? I'd screamed all that and much worse when he and Mom put up a united front against me holding it at all.

But it wasn't like I was the only one who had changed for the worse. When I first met Peter at age six, he had been a breath of fresh air. Okay, so maybe not so fresh because he smoked, but he brought adventure, new perspectives, humour, and fun into our lives. He wooed Mom with romance and passed his love of Monty Python, Asterix and Obelix, and Seinfeld onto me. He did goofy, exciting things like make pizza from scratch, teach us field hockey, and dance-drive with the sunroof off, music blaring in his Volkswagen. As the years passed these occurrences became rarer. By the time I turned ten I would have to beg him to watch Flying Circus or dance-drive. By thirteen, we barely spoke to each other, and when we did, we screamed. Fun Peter had died and a condescending tyrant had taken his place.

A few weeks ago, during our family phone call, he had said, "You're a smart young woman, Léa, what is the logic behind refusing to brush your teeth?"

"Calories. Duh." Toothpaste had flavour which meant it had calories and I was already on a meal plan of four thousand of them a day.

He asked if I wanted him to email Crest about how many calories were in a gram of their toothpaste. He was sure it must be less than five.

No. Five calories was still five too many. Unless he could get me zero-calorie toothpaste, brushing my teeth was part of my past.

While the windmill plate spent that night fired in the kiln, I spent mine in a deep, dreamless, med-cocktail-induced sleep.

I woke up soaked with night sweat, another med side effect that I ignored as I powered through jumping jacks. After breakfast, I flossed my teeth twice, then gargled with water, grimacing at the rancid, fruity, nail-polish-remover scent of my own breath. My hunger halitosis was even grosser than Peter's smoker's breath. Charlie, my favourite mental health technician, tactfully didn't mention it as he escorted me off-unit to Dr. Gill's office.

I liked Dr. Gill, but that didn't make me hate therapy any less. Upon admittance to UCLA neuropsych, sessions included filling out endless questionnaires and answering the Rorschach inkblot test. My dark responses, like two fat pigs dancing over a sacrificial fire for card #8, prompted my pairing with Dr. Gill, known for handling noncompliant patients with grace. She was also well-versed in the most effective therapy for OCD, exposure therapy. It means exactly what it sounds like: exposing a patient to what they fear in larger and longer increments until they build a tolerance to it.

Dr. Gill was super keen on doing exposures with the r-word. My aversion to it was one of the only elements of my OCD not related to exercise or religion. It's a testament to her kindness that she never once used that word or pushed me out of my comfort zone. Everything we did, I agreed to, like imaginal exposures where I performed compulsions and imagined that it was her doing them instead.

The day after Lupe left, the compulsions we targeted were

flicking on and off light switches. Obviously exercise. Our process included recording:

Thoughts Why am I doing this? Only a worthless weirdo gets bothered by light switches.

Feelings Extreme anxiety. Dread that surged through my veins, twisted my guts, and made my heart pound in my ears.

Distress Rating out of 100: 80. No, 90. Dr. Gill guided me through replacing these with . . .

Alternative Thoughts Doing this means I am closer to going home. It is hard but not the end of the world.

Alternative Feelings Resigned. Eager to get this over with so I could go home.

And a new Distress Rating out of 100 half an hour after: 70.

On December 21st, my distress skyrocketed to 350 out of 100 thanks to God punishing me twofold. First there was my blood blister, which I'd picked. The protective flap of dead skin that sheltered raw toe flesh hung on by a dermic thread. What hurt worse than the wound ripping when I stepped on it was the iodine that perpetually angry nurse Ron swabbed over its bleeding surface. He was merciless, rolling his eyes as mine teared in pain from the disinfectant's piercing sting. Misery I had earned, since I'd broken down and rested the night before during my jumping exercises.

That was why God had brought her back.

Justine.

"Léa, you're still here." She'd smiled upon seeing me, grin widening to something wicked. She'd cooed, "Remember the r-word?"

I would've rather downed a whole bottle of iodine than engage with her. My shaking legs launched me toward my old safe place. The bathroom. Except this time, the indigestion was real. My guts in knots from panic-induced diarrhea. It kept me up all night.

Since my first week at UCLA, Thursday was Weigh Day, and Weigh Day was Hell Day for every eating disorder patient.

First thing in the morning, clad only in paper exam gowns, we each had our date with the scale. But on Thursday the 22nd, the hospital's last day of regular scheduling, I was A: more worried by Justine; and B: somewhat distracted by Dr. Di Giacamo.

Masquerading as Santa, he had ho-ho-ho-ed his way into 2 South. The short, Italian man dressed in a red suit trimmed with white fur and matching hat was hardly convincing. The curly white beard he wore clashed with his dark eyebrows, and it was obvious that the white sack slung over his left shoulder was from a hospital laundry hamper. Not that any of us kids cared, what mattered were the presents inside.

The youngsters on the unit were happy with their Christmas-themed stuffies; Angel received an angel ornament she called her "Mini Me," and Justine stomped away in disappointment when the wrapping paper she'd ripped revealed a hair brush and comb set.

At first glance I couldn't tell what the tissue paper in my gift bag hid. I uncovered a soap and lotion set. The subtext: Léa, take more showers. I guess I stank. But I hated taking showers because they involved looking at and taking care of my expanding body. Too awful. I opened the liquid soap for a sniff, bracing for some overly sweet berry odour only to be met with pineapple and coconut. Not bad. There were worse things than smelling like piña coladas.

The next day, Friday the 23rd, I sat squished on the couch in the day room between Angel and Justine. Since there was no programming, we'd launched a Christmas cartoon marathon and were part way through Frosty. In a journal on my lap, I'd written "TGIF," Thank God it's Friday, in capital, 3D letters. While still angry at God, Dr. Gill said you can feel two opposing things at once, so I also gave thanks to Him. Especially for keeping my parents safe on their plane ride. A fact confirmed by their phone call.

Hyper-aware of the door that I always needed to open and close, I leapt up to do so anytime I heard footsteps nearby. Finally, I heard the confident click-click of high heels and Mom and Peter appeared through the wire-screen window. Angel high-fived me and whispered a quick "hi" to them. Justine glared and barked at us to be quiet. I complied, herding my parents off the ward and out of the building, not stopping until we were in the parking lot.

"You smell like my favourite cocktail," Mom murmured to me after planting kisses on my cheek. "Your teeth are a little yellow though."

Peter changed the subject. "Want to see our cool ride?" He pressed a key fob and a banana-yellow Mustang rental beeped to life.

"No way," I tried, and failed, to hold back a snort.

To make a car dance, jerk the steering wheel back and forth so that it wiggles on the road, shaking its wheels to the music. Dance-driving was what Peter did when he was happy. One third goofy flirting with Mom, one third being a Fun Dad, and one third showing off to the world. In the hospital parking lot, Peter blasted Van Morrison and made the car dance. All of us cracked up at the wide-eyed stares of strangers.

Then we hit the highways, driving around, seeing the sights, until I had to go back to UCLA for dinner.

It dawned on me that I had been wrong. Peter as a person was vast enough to be both dance-driver and condescending tyrant and maybe even some other selves in between. And if he had all these different sides to him, maybe other people did too.

After a Christmas Eve of shopping, avoiding Justine,

and a night of sweaty sleep, it was Christmas. All that was missing was a tree. At 2 South we didn't have one because it was a smash risk. When I first opened the door of Mom and Peter's Tiverton Hotel suite, there was a TV on a dresser but no sign of the Christmas tree Mom had sworn she'd brought.

"Look again," she said, walking towards the tiny kitchen and dining room area. She pointed at the table with a flourish, where a box of Walker's shortbread and some wrapped presents lay beneath a tiny, one-foot fake pine.

"It's our very own Charlie Brown tree!" I cheered, then caressed its stiff plastic needles.

Trunk straight and artificially verdant, adorned with tiny lights and gold ornaments, it was in remarkably good condition for having been squished in a suitcase.

I flushed, more in shame than pleasure, after counting my numerous gifts. All I had to show love back were meagre handmade offerings. Mom "oohed" over her rose soap, which she insisted on using immediately. Meanwhile, Peter slowly turned his windmill plate all the way around, as if trying to find an alternate use for it after I'd told him it was decorative, not for eating.

"Hope you like it, Pete," I broke the silence.

"It's great." He replied, clapping me on the back after giving me a hug. "I'll put it in my study."

I unwrapped my bounty so carefully that the wrapping

✱

paper could be reused. My favourite present was an MP3 player Mom had filled with hits like "Hollaback Girl" and "Don't Funk with My Heart." I'd also received some thick fantasy paperbacks, a journal, and a silver butterfly necklace. Then there was my least favourite gift, an electric tooth-brush and Crest toothpaste tied to a folded piece of paper with a ribbon.

"Just read it," Peter said.

I rolled my eyes as I ripped the curlicued ribbon apart—not wanting any of this packaging preserved—to reveal an email.

Hi there Mr. van Engelen,
Thank you for contacting Crest!
Every one of our Toothpastes contain 0.12 calories per brushing. This is not meant for ingestion and if it is swallowed caloric content is minimal.
I hope this helps!
Marya
Crest Team 7254

"See, barely one tenth of a calorie that you end up spitting out." Mom emphasized the last two words as if I'd forgotten how teeth brushing worked.

"Not barely one tenth, over one tenth." I didn't quite snap. "I'm sticking with water."

Peter glared back at me and opened his mouth, but before he could speak Mom cleared her throat, "Speaking of water, who wants something to drink? I'm getting thirsty, are either of you thirsty?"

While Mom opened the fridge and Peter found cups, I bagged up my hoard and put it by my shoes. Next, I cleared away the wrapping paper and gift bags, tucking the toothpaste in the garbage with them. Then, I let myself relax with Diet Vanilla Coke. I took long draughts of it. Mom drank eggnog. Peter spiked his with rum. He was full-on snoring by the time Mom and I migrated to the king-sized bed to watch *Elf*. When Will Ferrell got all of New York singing carols, my pass was almost up.

"Don't be sad, sweetie." Mom's arms around me slackened as mine squeezed her tighter. "We'll see each other tomorrow."

It would have been b-e-t-t-e-r if we hadn't.

The day after Christmas was a Monday and I had risked Justine's wrath by turning down her offer to play badminton. Even though she had suddenly professed the urge to diet, she'd yet to take sports or calorie-burning seriously, which meant I would have been left standing as she chatted instead of serving the birdie. Instead, I did ab exercises for an hour in my room.

She caught up with me in the living area and jabbed me in the solar plexus, "You're a bad friend. You abandoned me. I hate y—"

"You have a point." I cut in before she said any more, fearing the worst from her. "What if I made it up to you? I could draw you in a Christmas costume or draw you as a Disney princess."

"Make me a superhero, then maybe I'll forgive you," she said, tugging me to the art table.

My first sketch was sloppy and rough. No wonder she ripped it. But when she crumpled up my second, more realistic versus overly cartoony, I bit my lip to hide my frown. The third sketch I took my time on, beginning with the faintest of construction lines. It was shaping up to be pretty good.

"Erase it again." She pointed at the curve I'd made to form her belly, grimacing.

I looked at her, then at the drawing, with proportions I'd skewed slimmer than accurate. "Why?"

She scowled. "Too round."

"Still?"

"Yes, still."

I sighed and looked to the clock on the wall. Mom would come to get me in about ten minutes.

"What's so special over there?"

"Nothing. I was just checking the time because my pass is soon."

"So, you're abandoning me? Again?"

Patience left me as I attacked my drawing with an eraser.

"Don't tell me you wouldn't take the chance to get off unit if you could."

Justine's scowl deepened to a glare. "That's . . ." she paused, "not . . ." paused again, "right!"

I cringed. "Please don't say that word. I'll finish your drawing, I promise. Then we can play Go Fish when I get back."

"Fine. You better come back quick." The b-word seconds after the r-word was like being hit when you're down. I forced my shallow breaths to lengthen and reminded myself that she didn't know about the b-word.

"How about this?" I drew a concave line where superhero Justine's stomach should've curved out.

"I guess that works. Now draw me in cool boots."

"High heels or no heels?"

Justine took her sweet time deciding on thigh-high wedges, getting me to erase and redraw their length. Ten minutes became five. I was finally, finally done drawing the left boot when someone knocked on the door. My mom had arrived.

"Hey Léi Léi, baby, let's go."

Justine snapped, "You can't leave yet. You're not done."

My hands trembled and I had to erase the wonky lines they made. I begged Mom, "Give me a few minutes."

She shook her head no. "Peter's double-parked. He'll get a ticket."

Justine wouldn't budge. "You promised you'd finish."

✲

I drew for another few minutes, frantically explaining my promise to Mom, who tapped her foot with impatience. "Just finish it later."

"There." The pencil clattered on the table as I dropped it to stand up.

Justine's hot hand pushed me back down. "You still have to colour it. It's not finished."

"Colouring wasn't part of the deal." Now I was the one arguing with Justine as Mom flipped open her ringing cell phone. Peter yelled over crackly airwaves about a traffic cop, swearing in Dutch.

"You said you'd finish it . . . right?"

Adrenalin flooded me with fight-or-flight energy. Fight mode spewed out, "And I did! Don't blackmail me."

"You're wrong. You didn't finish. I'm right. I'm right, Right, RIGHT!"

"Shut up!" I clamped my hands against my ears and leapt so fast from the chair that it fell. The thud of it hitting the floor, a distant clang against my thundering heartbeat. I squeezed my ears as hard as I possibly could, welcoming the pain.

Everybody was staring at me.

Mom flipped the phone shut and snapped, "What the hell's going on?"

I lifted my hands away from the sides of my head and buried my face in them so no one could see my tears. When

I did look up again, I locked eyes with Mom. "Get me out of here."

Mom grimaced, frustration winning over sympathy. "You better tell me what's going on."

The other word. From the person I loved most. I screamed. Only aware of my need to escape. I didn't stop until I slammed the door to my room and buried myself under the bedsheets.

Nine hours later, someone else's anguished cries woke me. I stumbled to the Nurses' Station to ask who was dying. Ron jerked his shaved head towards Justine's room.

"Bad dream or something. She said I was making it worse."

Fucking Justine, ruining the night as an encore to this morning. I rapped on her door. Hard. "Give it a rest. None of us can sleep because of you."

The wailing continued. The only word I could make out was "nightmare."

"You deserve it for being so horrible earlier!"

The wailing stopped.

I leaned my ear against the door, straining to hear what Justine was saying. It opened and I fell onto her.

"Y-you think I deserve to get caught by them?" She asked as we disentangled in the dark of her room, both getting up from the floor.

"Them who?"

"The shadow monsters."

"Huh?"

She grabbed my arm and dragged me to her bed, then pointed at the opposite wall. "See, there, the scary shadows."

Sure enough, a large swathe of darkness loomed against the wall.

Looking at it again, she started hyperventilating. "They're gonna, they're gonna eat me. They won't while you're watching. But you're gonna leave, you always do. And then they'll eat me." She hugged herself and shivered.

I could have used the monsters against her, proclaimed that they would definitely eat her unless she promised to never ever say the r-word again. I could have harnessed her fear to make her feel as miserable as she had made me. Sweet, vengeful justice and a chance at future safety. I considered it.

Justine curled in on herself, head hung as her trembles intensified. She was so young and so scared and so vulnerable. A child whose mind had run away with her. At the mercy her darkest thoughts. I knew all about that. I breathed deep and on the exhale, released that pain so it couldn't hurt either of us anymore. "No, they're not going to eat you, and I'm not going to leave you."

I turned on the light. We both blinked as its brightness revealed the standard issue closet each room had in the corner. Half open with the light off, from her vantage point it resembled an open jaw ready to devour her. "It's just your wardrobe."

"Oh."

"Now that you know what it is, don't scream or cry anymore, okay?"

"Okay."

"Good."

Before I could leave though, Justine had grabbed me again. This time to squeeze me in a long hug. She rested a round cheek against my bony shoulder and some snot from her nose got on my shirt sleeve. I didn't care. Her soft arms squeezed me with more strength than I'd figured a twelve-year-old would have. After a few more sniffles she lifted her head.

"I forgive you for not colouring the picture of superhero me. Anger's tricky. It makes you feel strong like you don't need anyone, but that's a lie. Friends need friends."

Yes, they do.

Tiara

JOLÈNE SAVOIE-DAY

In 2008, I planned the biggest party I'd ever thrown. I invited a mix of high school and university friends, sorority sisters and ex-boyfriends, colleagues and my parents. People would be flying in from Toronto, New York, and Nashville. My "Dirty Thirties" birthday party was going to be epic. It had to be.

If you took a snapshot of my life at that moment, it looked great. I had a good job and owned a car and a house. I travelled, had fun, and was surrounded by amazing friends. I presented myself as a strong, independent woman who could stand on her own—or at least appear that way—because sometimes you have to fake it until you make it. Eventually, if others believe it, maybe you will too.

I looked for validation in my relationships with men. I wanted to be told I was beautiful, witty, and smart. I wanted to appear successful, appear put together. Appear happy.

Ask anyone, they'd say I was exactly all those things. But I'll admit I wasn't so sure.

Nevertheless the show must go on. I asked guests to dress up and bring slippers. I bought a sign that said, "Please remove your shoes and don't take a better pair when you leave." At MAC I got my makeup done. At home I dug out a navy-blue velvet box from the closet shelf, which contained a Swarovski necklace and matching earrings, and placed it on the dresser beside Kerrie's wedding tiara, an arch of delicate snowflake-like crystals.

Kerrie and I had worked together supervising tour guides on Parliament Hill. I was there when she married her high school sweetheart surrounded by friends and family. The party was loads of fun and she looked fantastic in a gorgeous fairytale ballgown and her sparkling tiara. The wedding was perfect until Stacey, another co-worker, stepped on a piece of broken glass while cutting a rug and smeared a trail of blood across the dance floor.

The love of my life, Nick, and I drove her to the hospital, checked her into emergency, and got in a fight in the waiting room. Stacey was fine, but Nick and I didn't go back to the wedding. We broke up two months later, moved out of our apartment, and closed our joint bank account. We stayed friends, however, which wasn't easy because I thought he was the one as far back as my twenty-fifth birthday. He was handsome, fun, and gregarious. We would host get-togethers with a good number of friends and we would dance the night away. I'd make a signature drink of vodka martini with crème de cacao, Kahlua, and peppermint Schnapps. Being part of a power couple, I felt mature, elegant, and loved. I was on my way and I knew I'd have an established career, get married to Nick, travel, buy a house, and have a baby by the time I was thirty. Until we broke up, I thought I had this in the bag.

My dreams of wedding days with a white mermaid gown, bedazzler-level jewels, and shimmery shoes were fed by movies like *Sleepless in Seattle* starring Meg Ryan and Tom Hanks, whose characters fall in love at the top of the Empire State Building, and *The Little Mermaid*, where Ariel marries Prince Eric in a glorious ceremony by the sea. And then there were my parents, who "fell in love with each other on the first date" and married young, and I always thought, in my own way, I'd follow them on a similar path.

Now, entering a new decade, having survived a couple of setbacks, I really wanted—no, needed—to be the belle of the ball. I needed a tiara.

Kerrie said yes right away and she was happy to play a part in making my day special. She said to ask for one was a very "Jolène thing."

My mom called me "princess" the day I was born. It was in the middle of a snowstorm and my family celebrated Christmas two days later. She always said I was her early gift.

For the first seven years of my life, I had no problem with Jesus and me having a birthday in the same week. But just before I turned eight, everything changed. We moved away from my dad's extended family and Shediac, New Brunswick, the lobster capital of Canada and where my Uncle Michel was mayor.

Up to that time, I had spent all my life with my cousins, aunts, and uncles. As the youngest among the Savoies, my birthday was a big deal. Once, Aunt Denise spent hours making a chocolate cake shaped like a Christmas tree. I destroyed it with my chubby hands and ate it by the fistful, leaving nothing for my older, salivating cousins. In the summers, I splashed in Aunt Denise's inground pool, built sandcastles at Parlee Beach, and ate vanilla twist ice cream dipped in rainbow sprinkles. Living among them made me feel accepted, loved, and that I had a place where any of my dreams could come true.

I was heartbroken when we moved to Ottawa. The two cousins I had there were way older than me. There were fewer aunts and uncles. I didn't know the mayor. On the first day of Grade 3 at my new school, I had to stand up, introduce myself, and say where I was from. I was so nervous, I forgot the name of my previous school, said the name of the current one, and everyone laughed. The teacher pointed out that I had an accent and asked me to say more things. I didn't understand why and thought they were laughing at me. What was funny about being Acadian? I felt lonely and homesick.

A few months later I turned eight. I don't remember that

*

first Ottawa birthday, or if I had a party. But I know that's when the problems started. My Ottawa classmates never sang to me, not enough friends and cousins came around, and, most importantly, everyone except my mom thought it was okay to smoosh my birthday with Jesus'. I received birthday presents wrapped in Christmas paper. So while the Son of God died on the cross for our sins, at least He never received combined gifts. "This is for Christmas AND your birthday!"

I also felt bad for having a birthday that was such an inconvenience to others. I didn't ask to be born on December 23rd! Was it wrong that I became vocal about wanting my birthday to be treated as such, not like some kind of half-assed merger, where one holiday awkwardly gets shoved up the ass of another, like a turducken?

My mom says I developed rules about how His birthday had to take a backseat until I had mine. She knew not to put up any decorations or have them visible anywhere in the kitchen or living room until I had my party.

Six months after my eighth birthday, I developed a powerful homesickness that would hit me in the middle of the night. While camping at Camp Kateri with the Jeanettes (French Girl Guides) near Ottawa, I was fine during the day—cheerful, surrounded by friends, and having fun. But at night, it felt like a mask fell away, revealing an intense ache that kept me awake. I was lonely. I missed home. I cried quietly in bed, though my emotions shook the bunk I shared with another camper. I was inconsolable.

The counsellors tried to talk to me, but I couldn't speak. They invited me into the kitchen, where a late-night crew was making Rice Krispies treats, and just like that, my tears stopped. I was back on track, playing the role of the happy child. The next day, I acted and felt as if nothing had happened, but the nightly crying continued. When my parents picked me up at the end of the week, the counsellors said they'd never seen a child cry so much. The feeling would overwhelm me whenever I was away from *Mame pis Pape*. I was consumed by helplessness, a lack of control, and the uncertainty of the future. The only thing that stopped the tears was being fully awake, out of bed, and back on stage.

I slipped on a floor-length backless black dress with cocoa-coloured sequins and spritzed on J'adore by Dior, which smelled like ylang-ylang, orchid, and mandarin. I carefully placed my friend's tiara between my bangs and hair pouffe and applied a generous amount of Sebastian Shaper Hold and Control. I put on sequinned ballerina flats and, for the final touch, a white satin sash with tiny scarlet stars and bold black letters announcing "Birthday Girl."

I glanced in the mirror one last time. I was looking forward to my thirties. And all I needed was for there to be, under no circumstances, a repeat of what happened the year before, on my twenty-ninth birthday. All I had to do was keep everything under control.

I took a swig of champagne and left the bedroom. It was go-time.

I crossed the hallway and stepped into the living room, where twinkling lights framed the windows, silver and gold decorations hanging like snowflakes in winter. The lights weren't red, yellow, or green, but they still felt festive— because I'm not the Grinch. I had come to realise that if you can't beat them, join them. Christmas wasn't going any-where, and I wanted to embrace the season. I wanted people to enjoy themselves, not tiptoe around my birthday.

The coffee tables were neatly arranged with snacks, coast-ers, and napkins, ready for guests to enjoy. I'd found them at Leon's and loved that they had wheels, were L-shaped, and could nest together to create a spacious surface—perfect for when I painted my toenails, though no guest needed to know that. The pair had been pushed to the side, revealing pockmarks on the light hardwood floors. They were only visible in the daylight, and no one noticed them until I pointed them out. I couldn't unsee them. They were small divots that were too deep to sand down. They clustered around the living room couch, the dining room table, and in between both spots, a *chemin* of craters. There were hun-dreds and in the course of the next 365 days, they seemed to multiply on their own, like acne on a teenager's face. They were reminders of the crap that went down last year, each an emotional scar on my heart.

The bash for my twenty-ninth birthday was my first big party in the house I'd bought with Gabriel, my first serious relationship after breaking up with Nick. It seemed like a good idea at the time. Before the house, we lived on the second floor of an old duplex in the dodgy part of the Byward Market with a roommate who was a chef in an upscale restaurant. At first, things were great there. Gabriel would bring me coffee in bed, serenade me to Dave Matthews Band songs on his guitar, and dance with me every morning to The Weather Network music. You know the tune—it plays in a loop when you're checking the daily forecast, and what's going on in Ottawa, Gatineau, and Kingston. He used to say the elevator music was "our" song.

Then, the honeymoon phase ended. We bickered and fought, and Chef Roommate, who'd known Gabriel before I did, started to hate me. Plus, we found just outside our doorstep too much sex trade and too many needles and— the worst—tourists. I tried to stay positive, went to therapy, and read *The Art of Happiness* by the Dalai Lama. Great guy, but it didn't work.

Gabriel had an epiphany. He saw us buying a house and making a fresh start. The idea went against my cardinal rule: never buy property with a man who isn't my husband. (I have so many rules. I'm a rules girl.) But our current living conditions sucked, and I felt stuck. The last straw was when Chef Roommate seared steak in butter at midnight. The smoke filled our loft bedroom, the alarm went off, and she didn't share. That would have been fine, I suppose, except the next day, I smelled like a fajita. At work, I created an MLS account.

Our house-hunting efforts landed on the place I still live in: an adorable red-brick bungalow built in the sixties. I remember visiting it at the end of the day when the sun flooded the living room. There was no furniture, and the freshly refinished hardwood floors gleamed. I wanted to slide on them and imagined us dancing to The Weather Network tune in our new home.

We signed the papers in early July and would take possession in two months. Before that, though, I had to go to Victoria, BC, for a summer residency at Royal Roads University's Masters in Leadership. The focus was to develop our skills and capacities to lead self, others, and organizations through complex change. And that's where I started to do academically-directed self-exploration. I wasn't looking for it, but I had to do it. I drafted vision and mission statements, reflected on my personal motivations in life. I took walks in the woods, and sat on giant rocks overlooking the ocean, overwhelmed by a sense of panic. Was I doing the right thing buying this house with this man? He could be manipulative, emotionally immature, and so negative. He said I was the love of his life, but he was also flirty with other women. Besides, was he really the love of mine?

During my time in Victoria, there was this guy in my program who usually sat at the back. We hadn't chatted much. Then one day, he sat beside me at the pub. Our connection was instant. His name was Liam and he was from Ottawa, too. We shared wings, walked back to the dorms under the stars, and talked for hours. I was smitten. In the last days of classes, Liam and I sat on the stairs that led to Hatley Castle on campus, the one you see in the X-Men movies. It overlooked the Pacific Ocean on one side and colourful botanical gardens on the other. We kissed at sunset. I felt like I'd found my Prince Charming.

I wrote a breakup speech on the flight home. Before I could really get into the delivery, Gabriel told me he also had doubts, fears, and a sexy coworker named Crystal waiting on the side. Before the end of the summer, we broke up, transferred ownership, and I moved into a house I loved with a mortgage I couldn't afford by myself.

My parents were concerned. They checked in on me, brought food, and avoided talking about the breakup. I had a therapist for that and a week later, I was there crying, feeling depressed, and questioning my life choices. I babbled about the power of positive thinking. Why wasn't it working for me? I had even brought my journal:

I have to stay positive, be grateful for what I have, and

keep my focus on what I want. I want to be happy. I
want to be in love. I want to be stable. I want to be
fulfilled. I want to live life to the fullest. I want to learn
from my mistakes and for setbacks to be lessons learned.

The leaves turned bright shades of red, yellow, and orange, and the hot and heaviness of my relationship with Liam cooled down. He suffered from depression and anxiety, and revealed he was a closet introvert. I was not an outwardly crass person, but "Fuck my life" crossed my mind.

He went on to explain he thought we were moving too fast, said he had doubts, and was convinced he would disappoint me. I was hurt, annoyed, and started to think my expectations of him were too high. I was terrified he would break up with me, so I acted nonchalant.

That's when Gabriel reached out to talk. He still loved me, wanted to make things work, and to move into "our" house. My mind was spinning and that was my state of mind as I tried to host my twenty-ninth birthday party, a week before my actual party (because who shows up to a birthday bash two days before Christmas?), in the dream house that was turning into a big hassle. *Ah ben coudonc, tant pis.*

"*Salut, entrez!*" I said.

"*Bonne fête, princesse!*" my mom said. She handed me a crockpot with homemade Swedish meatballs.

"Where can I put this?" My dad followed carrying another slow cooker with tiny sausages in *moutarde de meaux*.

"On the kitchen counter. Boots on the newspaper and coats on the bed in my room."

The doorbell rang some more and from then on it was a steady flow of double kisses, bear hugs, and pink gift bags. I spent my evening fluttering about, happy as a social butterfly. Maybe twenty-nine wasn't going to be so bad.

We ate, laughed, and at the end of the night, I sat on the floor opening one thoughtful, birthday-only present after another. I loved being surrounded by tissue paper and friends, feeling bubble-wrapped with love. Then I grabbed my drink and stood up. It was my favourite part of the night.

I raised my glass and paid tribute to friendship, birthdays, and even the holidays.

Did I mention Liam was there? Him showing up was a good thing. He made an effort and showed that he cared. He almost didn't come because he had a cold, but he did, even if he walked around red-nosed, congested, and miserable. I was so happy. Maybe we still had a chance? And then he used his cold as the perfect excuse to leave. I had thought he would spend the night.

The next morning, I woke up to a messy kitchen, sticky floors, and a pounding headache. I was glad I'd set the coffeemaker. I wrapped my hands around the warm mug, inhaled, and took my first sip. I told myself it was a great party. Everything was going to be okay.

I opened the blinds to let in the sun and sat on the La-Z-Boy couch my parents had given me when I moved out. I brought my legs up and looked for a blanket. The floor was a mess I'd tackle later.

That's when I saw them.

I got up, walked over and moved a sheet of pink tissue paper.

"What the fuck? *Osti de câlisse de tabarnak!*"

Okay, I lied about not being crass, but I was tired, hungover and had no more coping skills. There, on my gorgeous, brand new hardwood floors: dozens of small dents the size of peas. I followed the pockmarks from one cluster to another and another. They were everywhere.

I spotted a bottle of Bailey's on the counter, poured a generous splash in my coffee, and gulped. What fucking lesson did I have to learn from this?

Who would have dared to wear pointy stilettos at a house party? Only a fashionista psychopath.

In the days leading up to my actual birthday, I made a mental list of potential suspects and toyed with the idea of buying a rug. I was angry at myself for allowing guests to wear footwear indoors. It was eating me up. I decided the culprit must have been my friend's visiting out-of-town aunt who had given me a citrus zester wrapped in Christmas paper. I tried to let it go.

A day before my birthday, Liam came over, our status still up in the air, and he spent the night. I woke up on the 23rd next to him, happy not to be alone on my special day, even though he gave me anxiety, and, I'm pretty sure, a case of strep throat. We had coffee, and he surprised me with a heart-shaped crystal tealight holder, which I took as a clear sign—but then he left at noon. I thought we were going to watch movies together. He said he would go home, change, and come back. A few hours later he called to say he couldn't come to my family birthday dinner because he had diarrhea. What the actual fuck?

I put on a brave face, dressed up nicely, and paid extra attention to my hair and makeup. I met my family at Lone Star. They asked me where Liam was. I told them he was sick, but my face must have revealed that I was annoyed. I tried to cheer up. Lone Star is Tex-Mex and serves fajitas in simmering cast-iron skillets, unlimited chips and salsa, and fishbowl Cadillac margaritas. It was the least Christmassy restaurant I could think of and I stood on a chair wearing a giant cowboy hat while disgruntled servers sang "Happy Birthday" to me. I decided he wouldn't ruin my birthday.

I spent December 24th with my parents watching the *La petite vie* Christmas special and eating Chinese takeout. They suggested I spend the night since they were hosting the next day. I said no but didn't tell them why. I didn't want to be helpless like a child in my childhood bedroom. If I was going to be alone, I'd do so like a grownup.

I listened to holiday music on the drive home, focused on the snowy road, pulled into the driveway, got out of the car, and checked the mailbox by the front door. I found a thick red envelope. I took off my boots, dropped my coat on the couch, and sat down expectantly. Inside was a letter and a CD. On the album cover was a glamorous shot of my friend Nicole with big hair and a bright smile, wearing a white feather boa in a hazy glow. It was intentionally over-the-top, like late-1980s Céline. I couldn't wait to listen. Her energy was exactly what I needed.

I poured myself a generous glass of Shiraz, drew a bubble bath, and lit candles. After grabbing a book, I slipped in the tub, and let Nicole envelope me in her beautiful, soulful, and sometimes out-of-tune voice. I felt connected and loved. When I heard the first chords of "*Minuit Chrétien*," a lump formed in my throat and tears welled in my eyes. I put my book down and allowed my emotions to follow the crescendo of the song.

I wasn't going to be okay. I didn't know what was going to happen. I didn't know if I was going to keep the house or have a boyfriend. Would I be married by the time I was thirty? Was I going to accomplish the things I thought I would?

My positivity bubble burst all over my bathtub. I watered down my Shiraz with tears. I sobbed for my failed relationships, unachieved goals, and the pockmarked floor. I was devastated by the state of the floor, knowing it was trivial, yet I couldn't get over it. I felt lonely and disheartened, like Bridget Jones in that scene where she has a total meltdown while belting out "All By Myself." I felt like I was back in Camp Kateri. If I had no control over the hardwood in my own home, what control did I have in life? My bath grew cold. I dragged myself to bed and I woke up Christmas morning feeling emotionally hungover. I made myself coffee, played Nicole's CD, and took down decorations.

In the next twelve months, I rented the spare bedroom to cover the mortgage, tried to see myself as a strong, independent woman, and let go of the ideas that had driven me for the last ten years. Clearly none of that had happened. I was okay with that. Truly. I had a rich, full life on my own. That's what I was celebrating at my Dirty Thirties birthday party.

The doorbell rang, I danced across the hall and opened the front door.

"Hey you," I said. "You made it!" Funny how even after a year of being friends, Liam still made me feel nervous, excited, and flirty.

"You know I wouldn't miss your fabulous party," he said, cocking his head to the side. "Nice tiara."

I curtsied.

"Here's a little something I got you—not in Christmas wrapping." He handed me a sparkly pink bag.

"You know me too well," I said, feeling flushed. "You can leave your boots on the newspaper and your coat in the bedroom, I'm just checking on something in the oven."

I backed away. Damn. He was wearing jeans, a T-shirt, and a blazer. What can I say? Effort is sexy, and I was so distracted by him I burned my arm checking on the appetizers. I iced it with my drink and carried on with the night.

He socialized with my friends, helped clear dishes, and kept resting his hand on the small of my back. I played it cool and focused on hosting, chatting, and drinking.

I can't remember how we ended up in my bedroom. It's where I had put the coat rack and spillover boots. I don't know what came over me. I felt powerful as a queen, sexy as a vixen, and wanted to reclaim the "with benefits" part of our friendship. He agreed, eager to make my birthday wishes come true.

We were deep in our antics when Nick walked in and caught us hiding the Christmas pickle. He grabbed his coat, assured me it was fine, and left. I felt embarrassed, mortified, and relieved that I still had my dress on. I feel odd sharing this salacious detail with you, but getting on Santa's naughty list with a guy who still wouldn't commit to me felt like a bad decision on my part. I deserved more and wouldn't settle for less. Getting caught was my wake-up call.

But I also knew I wouldn't have done such a thing the year before. While I no longer felt in control of a future that would or would not have marriage and kids, I was grateful for what I had: a loving family, an amazing cast of friends, and a home I had created for myself—damn the hardwood.

I can't really remember what happened to Liam. It didn't matter anymore. I opened my presents, gave the toast, and we danced the night away. The tiara didn't fall off once.

Advent

LAREINA ABBOTT

I wanted to experience Europe in the winter. I craved beauty. I needed clarity. And so, I decided to take a year off from work as a naturopathic doctor in Calgary. One of my former residency students had graduated and was willing to cover my practice. My daughter, Zoe, was four years old, and I wanted to spend time with her before she went to school.

In Calgary, I couldn't tell why my life was falling apart. I was working so hard to be successful, to make enough money, to be a partner and a mom. I was exhausted. My medical practice was growing, and I loved my patients, but I felt like it was always hard. I had moved my clinic twice but still worked with conflict as a coworker. I had a great husband, but he was always gone to Europe, or China, or the United States for work, and with a new house and a young kid, we needed the money.

When you run your own practice, there are never days off, and I worried about my patients constantly. Despite working full-time, I did the lion's share of the parenting decision-making. I had gone back to work when Zoe was four months old as we couldn't afford otherwise, and she had been either with a part-time nanny or at playschool since. I had had a traumatic pregnancy, as my appendix burst after I gave birth and I became septic, and I had never recovered my health. I became angry, resentful of my husband and his freedom and his travel, and I hated being that person, but I didn't understand why I had to sacrifice my job so that his could be more successful. Slowly, I fell apart, pieces chipped away with each trip he took. I began to have panic attacks, which could take days away from me. You know what they say, you can change your hair, your husband, or your home, but not all at the same time. I'd had enough haircuts to know that I had to make a different choice. Things couldn't go on like they were, and so, I decided to change my home. If Zoe and I left for a few months, it would give Jason a chance to work as much as he wanted in the busy season, and me a chance to see if I could find a way out of the crazy life I had somehow gotten myself into.

This was before the days of Airbnb, and I searched around a sabbatical homes website for affordable, beautiful places to live in Europe that were empty in the winter. I found houses in France, Belgium, and Spain, and I offered them one third of the proposed rent in exchange for an easy and consistent tenant. I got one enthusiastic reply. A woman in a small town in Spain would love to have us at her house, a restored convent, in exchange for watching out for damage in the rainy season and not making any demands.

And so, I found myself one night in November in a busy

Madrid square hauling my luggage off of the bus from the airport with a giddy and goofy four-year-old trailing behind me.

I wandered around the square looking for the street where our hotel was located, as Zoe hopped from stone to stone. Evening lights exposed pockets of young adults in warm yellow for a moment before they moved on to their destinations. Daytime performers packed away equipment. Old men sat smoking on the fountain edges, faded in the dusk. I imagined their fingers stained tenaciously yellow.

My big black roller bag clip-clopped over the cobblestones as Zoe trustily plodded along behind me, pulling her own animal roller bag in one hand and holding her LeapFrog Leapster in the other. I loved being able to spend time with her even though we were so tired, and she seemed to be born to travel. It was hard always being away from her at work. I had a decision to make. I didn't know if I wanted to make her proud that I worked hard and had a successful career or if I wanted to just be with her.

In the hotel, I put her to bed and looked out the window as the evening transactions were beginning in the busy street below. It was a foreign landscape for me, and I was here alone. A creeping feeling of loneliness filled me. If Jason was going to be gone so much, I wanted to see if I could be more independent, but I was exhausted from travel-parenting, decision-making and the work of handing over my practice.

I couldn't believe that I was allowed to be gone from work. I was going to try to live in a foreign country on a whim, alone. What had I just done? I had left my home and my partner to try to figure out how to live again.

Zoe and I recovered in Madrid for a few days. For some reason, I had thought that Spain would be like Mexico, vibrant and boisterous. I'd studied medicine in Phoenix, and had worked with and seen Mexican people as patients, so I spoke mostly medical Spanish. But instead of extroversion, what I found in Spain was a deep pride, a reserve, a cautious kindness.

I took Zoe to the Prado museum where she drew pictures of *The Garden of Earthly Delights* and delighted the museum workers. We walked the stone streets and ate Spanish treats. Tradition seeped into me like molasses; there was old stonework and dark paintings, and beautifully dressed people engaged in serious chats. Sharing all this culture with a four-year-old is like sharing caviar with a monkey, but I hoped somehow that it would stay with her.

Southern Spain in the winter is like an inhale, a long slow deep breath in, a break, a respite. I've never experienced Spain in the summer. I imagine it's chaotic and hot, and beautiful of course, but the Spain I know is still and fresh and cold until you light the fire.

We took a train to Seville where we were going to stay until Christmas, inching our way into the south. Seville is the fourth largest city and the capital of Andalusia. It was the capital of Muslim Spain and the launching point for Spanish colonization of other countries, as it sits on the River Guadalquivir, which leads directly to the Atlantic Ocean. Due to the mixed occupation history, Seville has stunning architecture. It was the location of the filming for the kingdom of Dorne in *Game of Thrones*, and wandering around the city was like walking into history. The Alcazar is a Moorish Renaissance palace that you enter through blue and green tiled hallways. You walk through a series of courtyards, and then into the lush and miraculous garden. It is one of the most beautiful places in the world.

The apartment we rented was a two-storey two-bedroom, filled with the kind of furniture you can only imagine exists: a chair that looked like a velvet red shoe, a black plastic chandelier, a table made of some kind of exotic wood heavily coated in resin and in an 80s' thought-bubble shape. Nothing fit together and yet everything fit in a certain garish style. The cold tile was suited to the hot summer days but not to our November escapades. I looked over the French door balcony and watched young adults passing below me through the narrow street. Seville seemed to consist mostly of the young on their way to something.

The Christmas markets started early, wooden booths that filled the town squares. Now I understood what the "European markets" in Canada were trying to simulate.

Individual stalls sold Catholic wares, most of which I had no idea what their purpose was. There were also stalls of bread, chestnuts, wooden toys, and nativity figurines. Nothing was cheap or plastic. People flocked to the squares and we stood among them, fearlessly crushed in a type of communal joy resulting from the kind of human proximity that existed before Covid.

One Christmas fair took place under Las Setas, giant mushroom-like concrete structures that formed a canopy and held a restaurant you could walk up to. Camels spat at us from pens underneath the mushrooms and we waited our turn to have a chance at the Shrek bouncy castle. We bought braided bread and roasted chestnuts and wandered amongst the Roman statues and modern concrete.

Work stopped for the holiday season and so Jason met us in Seville close to Christmas Day. I waited anxiously in the vaulted train station as Zoe looked through toy shops. Relief flooded into me as he stepped off of the train. My experiment to be independent made me realize how much happier I was when he was around. But if he wasn't the problem, then I had to wonder if I was.

We celebrated in that apartment, cutting ornaments out of cardboard paper and stringing them up onto our paper tree with red ribbon. The gifts we found were well made and small, as when we returned to Calgary, we would still have to fit everything we had into the bags we came with. With

Jason back, everything was an adventure. I didn't let myself think about why I left Calgary, focusing instead on the joy and movement of experiencing the holiday season in a different country. The image I hold now of Christmas in Spain is quite different than back home with the green and red and mall shopping, and the furious drive to get gifts in time. Spanish Christmas felt more like a song with a healthy dose of eating at cafés.

Even though it was fun, and Spain was beautiful, I was still exhausted. My goal for the trip wasn't just to have an adventure. I had to figure out how to get my life back. If Jason wasn't the problem, what was?

We made our way to Jimena De La Frontera on January 4. The train south from Seville gave us a glimpse of low orchard trees in a rocky and rolling green landscape. Everything looked rich in the way that olive oil looks rich, satisfying and filled with nourishment. I wanted to just lie down in those hills, rest between the trees like fallen leaves. Once we figured out how to make connections between two train stations miles apart, the trip was fast and efficient.

Jimena De La Frontera is one of the oldest towns in Europe. It lay small and beautiful on the side of a hill, white-walled and brown-roofed. The train platform was at the bottom, and the road wound up towards the square, which is the only flat spot in the town. In the square, metal multicoloured fold-out chairs sat by café openings and children played soccer, and somehow avoided losing their soccer ball down the slopes. We walked up a slightly inclined cobbled street in the sun. There were no breaks between the houses, just slight differences in doors and balconies. We found out that the whole street used to be a convent, since lovingly separated by an architect into units.

Our house had a thick, arched, wooden door, and we entered a terracotta-tiled hall with a rich red carpet. On the main floor a kitchen, dining room, small living room with a fireplace, and a piano room surrounded a small courtyard that beckoned with plants, a table and chairs, and a cold pool. The second floor was an open space with high ceilings and thick wooden beams. Two bedrooms with gauze falling from the ceiling to cover the beds, and a bathroom with a clawfoot tub stood off to one side. A terrace opened into the courtyard. I'm not sure what grace allowed us to be in this place but the part of me that needed beauty sang in response as we walked through the rooms.

We woke the next day to the sounds of excitement in the streets outside. When we emerged from our house on the morning of January 5, the town was restless with preparation. In the square were more bouncy castles, this time SpongeBob-themed. Kids ran through the streets with sculptures made from strung-together cans; we followed as they converged into a noisy parade. Musicians played flamenco guitar as they walked. Jason took some cans from a recycling bin, found some string and made a small sculpture that Zoe could drag through the streets alongside the can-toting children of Jimena. We had awoken to a festival that celebrates Epiphany, the Three Kings Festival, *La Fiesta de Los Reyes*. The three kings were the Magi, the men who visited Jesus in the manger. In southern Spain, this is when the kids get their holiday presents, which are left in their shoes (ostensibly by the three kings) the morning after the parade. It was deafening, and exciting. The next morning Zoe woke to find some hastily bought presents in her shoes, a second Christmas, a new tradition.

Andalusia, southern Spain, had welcomed us, and we were gratefully there. Jason and Zoe were having the vacation of their lives, but now that the holiday was over, I grew desperate to be alone. I wanted days and days of solitude, I wanted not to think, not to take care of, not to consider. My deep need to please and help others meant that it was difficult to understand myself around other people. I needed to be alone to figure out how I could again become the person I used to be, that spontaneous, sensitive, goofy person that loved adventure. The price of clarity is selfishness.

And so when Jason left to go back to Canada, it was both a sadness and a relief. Zoe and I settled into a calmer living. I wanted to hire a babysitter for a few hours a day so that I could write, but my landlord explained to me that because we were staying for a while, we were considered residents, and so when school started Zoe was invited to join the other four-year-olds. No one in Jimena spoke English. It's not that they couldn't, it's that they didn't want to. We had been teaching Zoe some Spanish in preparation, but all of the sudden she was in school with all Spanish-speaking kids. As a child, Zoe would roll down car windows to yell hello at children walking on the street. She is extremely social, and so she thrived in school. After the first few days, Zoe's teacher spoke to me in Spanish and said that Zoe needed to know essential phrases. She gave me a list for Zoe to learn. We practised every night as she played with her dolls. The list gave me a view into what it was like to be in a Spanish kindergarten.

Can I go to the bathroom? *Puedo ir al bano?*

Do your work. *Has tu trabajo.*

Quit talking. *Deja de hablar.*

Zoe began to speak in Spanish phrases. Children are very motivated to talk to other children, and her desire fuelled her learning. The teacher was kind, beautiful, and tough, perfect for my exuberant child. Zoe glowed in the life that Spain was offering her, in a way that didn't happen in Calgary. Finally alone, I imploded as I turned my attention to my chosen deep dive, researching a novel on the Roman empire.

The days became a rhythm of simplicity. Wake, eat, walk my daughter to school down the hill along the stone roads in the misty morning. Wait with the other parents as the children are lined up and taken in. Shop in the street market or the store for bread, wine, cheese, fruit, and vegetables. Work in the morning researching my book and then writing in the room with the umber walls and the tile floors. Gather my daughter and play or walk. Eat dinner, put her to bed. Make a fire in the big stone fireplace. Drink a glass of wine as the sun goes down. I was in Spain, on sabbatical. I was lucky and on vacation. I had chosen this. This was part of the life I wanted to live.

But as I lived this beautiful existence, as my crazy Calgary life faded, as I spent more time alone, I could no longer distract myself from a deep uncertainty.

I wrote and I researched and I felt a calm that I had not felt in a long time. Because of this calm, a small thought began to surface, an unwelcome thought. The more time I spent alone, the more I could hear it. I ignored it at first. I made ratatouille. I took little trips. I played and walked with Zoe.

It wasn't one large event that made me notice. It wasn't the joy of Christmas in another country. It wasn't the boisterous parade of Epiphany. It was instead the absence of events. It was the quality of the air after all the holidays had finished. It was a fire that I built myself in the stone fireplace. It was the richly woven red and blue rugs on the tile floors.

One evening, after I stoked the fire, as I looked into the courtyard and the fading light, I let myself say it.

I didn't want to be a naturopathic doctor.

As I was finally alone, I could no longer lie to myself that I had not come to Spain because I was on vacation. I had come to Spain because I was a failure. I was a failure because, if Jason wasn't the problem, then I was. I had gone through eight years of post-secondary school, and I couldn't hack the stress of the job. This wasn't really a sabbatical year, it was me figuring out how I could possibly keep going doing what I was doing.

My sister once said that in our family we have to leave the country to get drunk for the first time. I imagine that this was the same thing. The shame of failure meant that I had to leave to admit it. The shame of failing was too great to do it in Canada.

I didn't leave my work to a colleague because I had planned it.

The pressures of my job were causing me to lash out, to party too much and to blame Jason for my unhappiness. I was both driving myself at work and then driving myself socially to make up for the fact that work never became easy. But I kept pushing, staying in a toxic clinic until I had a break-down, and ended up desperately casting around for a way to save face.

I wanted out.

But I had spent eight years getting my doctorate, and my identity was connected to this job. I wasn't a quitter; if I left my work, then I was a failure.

You see, growing up, failure was something other people were allowed to do. My family felt the ache of judgement deeply. Any shame my father perceived was met by the answer of my ringing successes. I was family pride personified.

We were moving houses, again? I won a speech contest.

My dad lost his business? I got better grades.

My mom was sick? I excelled in university.

Succeeding was my answer to our chaotic world. My dad was white, my mom was Métis, and they both grew up poor and proud. They were hardworking and they made themselves independent. The burden of judgement was always on us though, and I knew my parents felt it. We were fierce in our defiance of what was expected of us.

I recently spoke to Marilyn Dumont, the great Canadian Métis poet, at a Métis women's event in Alberta. She talked about that burden of judgement on Indigenous people, and said something like, "Growing up, that white gaze was always upon us. We wore our Sunday best every day because we had to, because we were watched more harshly than the other kids."

We never talked about being Métis in my family, but there was always that sense of needing to prove something to the other families. I look more white than my mother did; although I have her tanned skin, I have my dad's blue eyes, which makes me look more Caucasian. My older sister mimics the whiteness of my dad's line, she burns in the sun like white milk in a hot pan. But no matter our skin, we still feel the burden of our ancestry. That need to make money. That need to prove ourselves. We never talked about our problems in public. We never told other people if we needed money. We never relied on anyone. We were a team, and that was all that mattered.

I have friends who have no problem failing spectacularly, even humorously. They have a buoyancy to their failure that feels like a balloon in a festive crowd, drop and be bounced up again, over and over, held up by family privilege. It's easy to fail faster when you are allowed to do it over and over. I had no contingency plan. My parents were gone; I had no backup other than my husband and four-year-old kid. My decision to take a year off was looked down on by Facebook friends: how dare I stop work for a year? Even though I had worked since I was fourteen, even though I had worked through school, even though the entirety of our existence in Spain cost less than the price of just childcare per month in Calgary, I was judged for dumping the costs of our lives onto my husband. I cancelled my Facebook account, preferring instead to live my shame in secrecy.

The town of Jimena is old, and the Andalusia area has

a long history of diverse occupation. The woman down the street dug in her courtyard to build a pool. The workers first found Islamic stones, and then underneath that they found a Roman road, and even deeper, they found an ancient milling stone belonging to some long forgotten culture. Each piece of land has been owned a thousand times. There is some comfort that, in such a place, we are just momentarily on the land, that the land lasts, and we are temporary.

In Canada, I always felt the need to create something new, something from nothing. In Spain, I was allowed to just live and live lightly. Things did happen—the rains caused flooding in the house and all the carpets had to be taken out and dry cleaned, we had to move out for one week to accommodate a different booking, a neighbour brought us to some Roman ruins to help in the research for my book—but overall, it was a gentle waterfall of joy, one calm adventure after another.

I couldn't imagine not doing the profession that I had spent eight years studying for, but slowly I began to envision different ways of living, a way of living the way you wanted to. A woman in her thirties lived across the street from me. She was born in Britain and she spent most of her time in Africa working on a wildlife reserve. Her life was lived in no English-speaking countries. Her house was filled with air and plants. We sat on benches in the sun, calmly talking about choices. She had chosen a quiet life, a life filled with open spaces and physical work. A life different than what had been expected of her.

The truth came to me as we spoke. I had always tried to find a profession that would allow me to live the life I wanted. It never happened. The profession never transitioned to something easy. I loved my patients, but it was always hard. The last year had been especially hard. A patient whom I loved had died of cancer. I was just treating her for side effects of her medication, but we became close. She was resourceful and she fought and rallied and fought again, but she wasn't yet forty when she died. It rocked me. In addition to this I hated asking patients for money. I hated that naturopathic medicine in Canada was so misunderstood and controversial. I hated that I didn't have time to spend with Zoe as she got older.

But, as I spoke to my neighbour, I realized that things didn't have to be hard. In the calm that came post-Epiphany, I had found my epiphany.

At the end of the winter, I returned to Calgary as the snow was melting. I asked the woman who was running my clinic if she wanted to buy the practice and she said yes.

La vida es Buena, especially on days that include tapas.

Saint Jude's

ELIZABETH SOMBOUN

The tall room at Saint Jude's Ranch for Children near San Antonio had a Christmas tree in the corner. I think it was thirty feet tall. The fireplace was lit. All the girls were seated: me, Lianne, and Rebecca on the one sofa and Rosemary, Jennifer, and Margarita on another one. Connie on her own.

Miss Dorothy read aloud from a book, an anthology. It was something about God rescuing people. No, it was angels saving people. I don't remember the name of it.

I kept looking out the window into the dark and the rain. I missed the snow in Jersey. I imagined all of the decorations that I would have helped with, and these Cabbage Patch dolls that I had. I thought about my younger brother Clayton not being with me. "What is this? Christmas without him? What are they doing right now?"

I was eleven and a half years old. But I also wasn't.

Lianne, who was my roommate when I first arrived, had been in a gang. Since I arrived in June, she had taught me how to hotwire a car, snort drugs, and use heroin. She taught me everything you could know about sex. She was sleeping with a twenty-five-year-old guy. Lianne was twelve.

After the reading, I drank eggnog by myself. I continued

looking out the window. I tried to imagine what my Christmas future would look like.

Behind me, an outrageous number of presents flooded the room, but there was no smell of homemade cookies and the sentiment of me having someone to call "Mom" or "Dad." That made the tons of wrapping paper at Saint Jude's a little less beautiful.

I didn't want gifts. I wanted a mother and father and beyond that I needed to be with my brother Clayton, who was miles away and I would never see him again. I was living one of those TV holiday specials where the orphan looks out a gloomy window pane and longs for a family. In those movies, the orphan always gets one, but none, I was certain, would come up the winding drive for me.

I never felt more like a charity case.

Miss Dorothy came up to me. "What's wrong, Marianne?"

That was my name then.

I replied, "I don't know." That was my answer for everything. "I don't know."

She said, "You can talk to me about it."

I said, "I can't. I can't talk to you about it."

"Why?"

"It's just, it's just too hard."

"Well, you know, you're gonna get adopted."

Even though in my heart I desperately wanted that to happen, I replied, "I don't know if I want another family."

She replied, "Well, it doesn't matter what you want. It's if the family wants you."

When I was first adopted, Clayton was two and I was four. Gayle and Peter brought us to the Hilton by the Riverwalk in San Antonio and gave us brownies and ice cream. The best ice cream I'd ever had, triple stacked. We were in a suite and it was super late. I brushed Gayle's hair. The brush got stuck and she jumped up and down frantically, making my brother and I laugh hysterically.

Gayle and Peter explained they had been trying for many years to have kids and they simply could not. That's why Clayton and I were adopted. They told us they loved us so much and that we were chosen by them. And like the big oversized Hilton bathrobes, Gayle and Peter seemed like cozy people. But I couldn't wear the robe of love comfortably. People think love just falls into kids, but sometimes kids have to stretch themselves to want it, and for me, that would take a long time. Still, I decided these were the adults who were running my life now. I told myself this was fun. This was our next big adventure. I'd always been like that, the kind of kid who rolled with the punches. I would go with the flow of things.

At some point, I looked at Peter. I said, "I don't feel very good."

When I was living with my biological mom, there were

times I starved and lived off dog food. My stomach wasn't used to lots of food. I threw up all over the hotel bed and Gayle and Peter had to get the staff to bring us new sheets and stuff.

The next day we visited the downtown San Antonio courthouse. Clayton looked so cute. He had on these very cute little red shoes and cute little red shorts. His shirt was blue with Humpty Dumpty on it, but we didn't know that at the time. Gayle sang the children's song over and over and over again, and we had never heard it before. We kept asking her to sing it again and again.

After the courthouse, they took us to the airport. We boarded and took off, and when I ate on the flight I got sick on Gayle. She was wearing a silk white blouse.

Even though I was a preschooler, I just knew what she was thinking. "This is a really bad sign here. This is not what we expected."

We landed at JFK. I saw the Statue of Liberty, the Twin Towers, and the New Jersey Turnpike. We drove to Paterson, New Jersey.

The house was big and a few blocks from the Hudson River. There was a massive combined kitchen and dining room and then another separate dining room. I recall a huge scroll-top desk that divided two living spaces and when I walked around it, I found stairs that led to the bathroom, the master bedroom, another bathroom, and the room Clayton and I would share because, up to then, we had never been separated.

That night, we were each under our own blue sheets and quilted comforters. There was a nightstand between us, but we talked around it. We were so excited and I think everyone was also afraid on some level, we went on nearly nonstop. Gayle and Peter stayed in the room, half dozing on the floor, hoping we'd settle down. We didn't until around five in the morning.

Peter left. Gayle went to turn out the lights.

Now, I've always been an observant person and back then I saw the world in that detached, calculating way. My biological mother told me later in life a story about me. She said I was never little. When I was a toddler, she would get grownups to ask me stuff about politics, and they thought I was going to say cute responses and they would have a laugh over my stupid answers. My mother said, "No, you actually debated politics for fifteen minutes and you went back to eating like your McDonald's and French fries and stuff. Yeah, you were really smart. You were never a child."

So, that first night in Paterson, I knew that Gayle was not my mother, but she needed to feel accepted by me. Gayle wanted to be called "Mom." I decided I was going to make her day. I said, "Goodnight. I love you, Mom."

She knew automatically that there was something wrong with me. She decided I was a very broken little girl.

I had arrived at Saint Jude's at the beginning of the summer. I discovered they had people they called sponsors who would come by and basically rent out a child for the weekend during the summer. My sponsors were Jill and Jerry Solomon. I had met these people after being at the Ranch for about two and a half weeks.

Jill was of Italian descent. She stood about five feet, ten inches. She had long hair and very high cheekbones. Jerry was six feet. He had blue eyes, a beard, and wore a cowboy hat and boots most of the time. He looked like a construction worker. I ended up spending a couple of weekends with them and they had taken a curious interest in me.

The first time I met them red flags went off. I remembered Gayle telling me befoe she sent me back that the only people who would adopt me next would be people that were like seriously insane, that they would do like horrible things to me.

Jill and Jerry Solomon really wanted to adopt me and I was becoming afraid of them. I told my caseworker that summer I didn't want them to adopt me.

She asked, "Why"?

I said, "Well, let me put it to you like this. Gayle and Peter Ruffings couldn't afford to put me in residential psychiatric treatment. This family makes way less than the Ruffings. They're not going to have the means to take care of me, and I do not want them to adopt me."

The caseworker was taken aback by my response.

I added, "I want to be in a family where I'm the only child. I do not want them to have other children. This is what I want."

"You know, it doesn't work like that. It only works like that when you're the adult. It doesn't work like that when you're the kid."

She explained to me that the agency had started running the numbers. They were going to waive the adoption fee.

I said, "Please don't. Because if they cannot afford the adoption fee, they're not going to be able to take care of me properly. And, there is a really weird reason why they want to adopt me. Please, do not put me in with this family."

On one of my weekends with Jill and Jerry, we went to a mall. Jill had gone to the washroom. Jerry stayed with me and I felt terrified. I kept wondering, "When is Jill coming out?"

I was up against a glass railing and I couldn't escape. I started having a panic attack.

Jerry was talking to me about thieving, and I kept thinking, "Why are you talking to me about this? I'm not gonna, like, steal. You don't have to worry. I'm not gonna steal." I wanted him to back off. I needed him to back off, but he continued to lecture me.

I already knew they didn't like me. They didn't like the way that I dressed. They didn't like the way that I spoke. They didn't like the subjects I spoke about. Why were they pushing so hard for this adoption to go through? All that summer, I couldn't get the adults to actually tell me like what the frig was going on. Then I realized in a prayer meeting, they're adopting me because it's a purpose from God. They didn't really want me. They saw me as a project to be fixed. They wanted to show the world and their church what amazing Christians they were. "Look how good we are!"

I was standing by the window with Miss Dorothy and the Solomons flitting through my head when the boys, David, Wesley, Joe, Bubba, and Chris Thuma, a gorgeous one and the closest around my age, came back from their Christmas Eve outing. I became a brat and I taunted them. I said, "Haha, you guys missed out on the eggnog. And we actually got a story read to us and you didn't."

Since I had arrived at Saint Jude's, being the youngest, still playing with Barbie, and the only virgin among them, the boys had picked on me. I was always looking for a way to get back at them. This time it was, in my eleven-year-old mind, through eggnog and storytime.

Miss Dorothy stopped me.

"Marianne, you shouldn't have said that. That was very mean. You're making the other kids feel left out," she said. "You know, you're gonna be okay."

I said, "I don't know. I don't know if I'm gonna be okay."

I said, "I'm going to get back and see if there's any more eggnog."

She gave me a hug. I hugged her back but I felt nothing. There was just this hollowness in me that night.

The road to me being sent back was when I was seven years old and three years into my adoption. Gayle and Peter had a miracle. Gayle became pregnant.

The day she found out she was having a girl, Gayle pulled her wedding dress from the attic and began transforming it into a baptismal gown. Kristen became the star of Califon Drive. Clayton and I had become cheap substitutes of what they had really wanted: a child that held their genes. I knew the word "genes" because Gayle at times reminded me my genes came from a white trash biological mother.

By the time Kristen entered the family, I was already seeing psychologists. I would hear them tell Gayle, "Well, your daughter is severely detached and detached kids usually end up being serial killers, and they usually commit murder by the time like they're twenty-one. Or she's gonna end up committing suicide by like the age of fourteen."

This was the state of New Jersey therapy.

But I want to explain something here. My very first psychologist, I don't remember her name, had an amazing house. She didn't live there, but her office was set up like a home and she used to wear these really cute outfits and had nice perfume. I remember thinking I'm here because they think I have problems and I tried to think my way out of the situation.

She wanted to know about my gory nightmares. I was, like, I can't. I couldn't tell her because they were about my biological mom. I believed Gayle would feel jealous and it would crush her self-esteem if I talked about my birth mother even though she had been a source of terror in those dreams.

I was always like that. I had a smartness or calculation that made trouble. The way my mind worked often alarmed Gayle and Peter. They often accused me of manipulating them.

I would reply, "I'm not manipulating you. I'm not being manipulative because you can't be manipulated by a child."

Their response was to start using a board to spank me, which left massive bruises on my body.

One time I had worn a skirt to school and a kid that sat next to me at my table asked me what happened to my legs, which were purple, green, black, and blue. I told him I just got a spanking, no big deal, whatever.

He told the teacher. The teacher called social services. Social services showed up at our door. Obviously, Gayle and Peter were furious. They accused me of trying to put them into jail. I told them I didn't tell the teacher, that another student told the teacher and they shouldn't have done what they did. Going forward, they felt they didn't have any way of disciplining me.

They considered sending me to a residential school, but they didn't want to pay for it. They figured I would go there, come back, and nothing would be changed. So then they decided to fight the adoption agency in San Antonio. They literally wanted a refund. Clayton had been $25,000 to adopt. I cost $10,000. A grand total of $35,000. I was the bargain because I was older. Plus they wanted me out of state. Gayle told the agency she was afraid that she was going to come and visit me or have any accidental contact with me because it would be too hard on her. Gayle and Peter claimed that they were very attached to me, and that sending me back was like the hardest thing for them to ever do.

But I think what they had was lots of pride. They were all about prestige, and what looks good to the outside world. They didn't want their former freaking adopted daughter around town after they had given her up.

The agency, Gayle, and Peter made a deal. My adopted parents had to send all my stuff, cover the flight back to Texas, and the agency would take me back, no refund.

At the end of Grade 5, I came back from school. I arrived at Gayle and Peter's grand two-storey house and found three massive storage boxes that held everything single thing I owned. The phone-book-sized pile of paperwork had been signed. I was an orphan again.

The next morning Gayle stood in the ornate family room, her eyes cloudy with tears and her cheeks hollow. She wouldn't come to the airport. Again, too hard. After words of remorse and choked up goodbyes, I rushed up the stairs one last time to say goodbye to my brother Clayton.

*

Clayton and I had never been separated before. I hugged him as if I could make my soul entangle with his. I kissed him and descended the stairs. My identity as a sister vanished.

Later that Christmas Eve night, Miss Dorothy gathered everyone around the fireplace for devotions. Then she gave a speech like it was a football huddle. "Everybody, it's getting late. You are going to go to bed. Chores have to be done Christmas morning. Once all of the chores are done, we are going to open the gifts."

Rebecca and Sabrina were my roommates. Rebecca was fifteen and slept on her own bed. Sabrina was closer to my age and slept underneath me. I had top bunk.

The hallways of Saint Jude's went dark. All of the kids were intent on going directly to sleep because nobody wanted to get in trouble that night. The house went super quiet. We whispered to each other—goodnight and Merry Christmas—and then they fell off to sleep.

And I just remember thinking, "What am I going to do?"

In the quietness, I thought about how much I liked Miss Dorothy and the mom-like feelings she gave when I was with her. I looked back at all the activities Saint Jude's organized for us during the month of December, just to prevent us kids from feeling the emptiness I felt that night and, frankly, offing themselves during the holiday season.

How were gift exchanges with Christian schools or meeting David Robinson from the San Antonio Spurs supposed to help me forget the pain of being forgotten?

I was soon to be twelve. I would no longer be considered a child. I would be seen as a teen. This was my last Christmas as a kid with only Jill and Jerry, the Solomons, wanting me.

My mind drifted back to a funder's holiday gala that all the orphans had to attend at San Antonio's Tower Life Building. It was a fancy terracotta building shaped in an octagon.

All of the adults dressed elegantly. The guys wore what I imagine now as their Hugo Boss suits. Everyone smelled amazing in perfume and cologne.

To me, they weren't just funders. They were potential families, so I had planned to go parent shopping. And I was comfortable in this sort of environment because Gayle and Peter used to take me to dress-up parties where Peter worked as a computer engineer.

I had all my clothes from home, so I wore my peach Jessica McClintock dress. It had a lacy front, puff sleeves, and more delicate lace at the bottom. It was one of the last dresses that Gayle had given me. I wore like black tights and white shoes to go with it. None of the other girls from Saint Jude's looked as nice as me.

I had figured that there were people at the gala who were dealing with infertility issues, who were looking for a child, that there was a family that was going to be interested in me especially after seeing me all dolled up like a porcelain doll. They were going to want to take me home. I had a plan.

They're gonna be rich and make me financially secure. I would have money for college, and I wouldn't have to share my parents with anyone.

I was very mannerly. I was very quiet, not my normal self, because I was trying to land a perfect family. I found them.

She was blond, with greenish-blue eyes and she was five-foot nine-inches tall. She was super pretty. He was tall and blond. I introduced myself, "I'm an orphan. Hello! My name is Marianne," I said. "How is your evening?"

They indicated it was going very well.

I said, "I'm very glad that you're putting this event on for us. It's such a pleasure, knowing that people are doing God's will for us orphans. Oh, by the way, like I'm adoptable, so you can talk to the woman over there if you want to adopt me."

They responded more or less with, "Okay, we'll talk about it and we'll see." I think they were just humouring me.

Before I could continue our conversation, Miss Dorothy grabbed me and peeled me away. "What are you doing?"

I said, "I'm looking for a family."

"Not at this event."

"What did I do wrong?"

"Come on, Marianne, let's just get you some food and sit over here and stop talking so much."

I said once more, "I'm trying to find a family."

Miss Dorothy sighed, rolled her eyes. "We will talk about this later. Just eat your damn food."

Strange. Thinking about Miss Dorothy there at the gala and being at Saint Jude's with her was like having a mom. She made me crave one.

I weighed in my mind what happens when you're an orphan and you're no longer a cute four-year-old. I thought about how I had been told by really horrible therapists and Gayle that my whole life would be doomed. They told me I would be beat up and raped to get into a gang at the group home. Maybe suicide would be a better option? I needed to get a family. Not the Solomons. But I couldn't be picky, because, like, I was aging really fast. I knew the next morning many presents would be waiting for me, but there would be no family.

If I don't get a family soon, I'm never going to get one.

As sleep took me, I talked to God. He didn't answer, not that night.

I decided to surrender to fate, to the Solomons, to allow them to have their way. I decided I was going to make the best of it.

Road to Ballyduff

SARAH EL SIOUFI

When I was around nine years old, my parents got divorced. Soon after, my father moved to Saudi Arabia for work. But Christmas, for a time, wasn't much altered.

My father had always been indifferent. On the morning of, he would be half asleep on the couch while my mom sat on our worn-out green loveseat, Turkish coffee in hand, with a tired smile. She'd watch me tear through my gifts. Once they were opened, I played with them for the rest of the day. So, when he was gone, the only thing that changed was that he was physically absent then too.

It was my mom who had bought the tree at Canadian Tire and lugged it home herself. She was the one who went to White Rose Crafts to buy the materials to make decorations. She surprised me with the tree trimmed in its red, white, and green ornaments. It was my mom who bought and wrapped all the gifts. She leaned into the fun.

Once I started school, my friends filled me in on Santa and I became fully immersed in the same batch of holiday cartoons that seemingly played on repeat for most of November and December, year after year. Mom's tree, in my mind, was just like the one in *A Christmas Carol*, the Mickey

*

Mouse version, which I had grown to love. The holiday made me giddy. I would practically vibrate with excitement on Christmas Eve. I couldn't wait to see if I would get everything I asked for.

I did, however, have a lot of questions about the logistics. "Will Santa come to our apartment even though we're Muslim?"

"Of course! Why wouldn't he?" my mom said.

How would Santa get into our condo when we had no chimney?

"We leave the balcony unlocked and he'll come through the door," she replied.

"What about the reindeer? They won't fit on the balcony."

"Well . . . Santa will park on the roof and an elf can help him down to each unit."

We were on the eleventh floor and Santa didn't seem physically dextrous. I was concerned.

My mom viewed Christmas as more of a cultural celebration rather than a religious one and knew that not letting me take part in the fun would single me out. There was no mention of Jesus. It was all about Santa, and I thought it was pretty cool that every December I got two weeks off school and a magic fat man brought me all the presents I asked for.

My mom tells me that I tried staying up all night one year to wait Santa out. I don't have a memory of it, but she says she found me sleeping on the faux-fur mat under the boughs.

As for Egypt, my memories are hazy. I was a toddler when I came to Canada, and I've blurred the line between genuine recollection and the stories I tell myself from old photos.

My *gedo* loved to share tales from the Qur'an in the most electrifying way. Animated and passionate, he made big gestures and changed his voice to suit the characters. I would sit cross-legged on the floor, chin in hand, captivated. I liked to follow him around the apartment in Giza when he washed for prayers, brushed his teeth, sipped his morning tea. My mom said out of everyone in our family, us moving away was the hardest on him.

My father's brother Ahmed had moved to Newmarket, Ontario, and opened a Dairy Queen. He was doing well for himself, and his success inspired my dad.

We ended up in Scarborough, which in my completely unbiased opinion remains the beating heart of Toronto. Home to multi-generational Canadians, it is also the first home to many immigrants drawn in by affordable neighbourhoods and an accessible-ish commute to the downtown core.

Growing up in Scarborough is an education in different cultures and religions with a huge variety of ethnic restaurants. The best ones are typically small, independently

*

owned and operated, with a rep built on word of mouth. It's arguably one of Canada's most diverse areas.

There are strip malls galore, packed buses with groups of kids who will cut you to shreds with smirks and judgemental eyes that snake up and down your body if you're ever having high notions about yourself.

Scarborough is hanging at Town Centre mall playing Mortal Kombat in the arcade, seeing a movie at the Coliseum, and loitering in the food court. It's having plans to ride your bike to Taco Bell to meet friends but having to take the TTC (bus) instead because it was stolen. There's much to be said for a place where not taking yourself too seriously or "keeping it real" is respected more than physical or material things and status.

But being there was a difficult adjustment. There were tensions and contradictions. We had left grandparents, cousins, aunts, and uncles to come to a vastly different country with only my uncle Ahmed in Newmarket and a second cousin in Mississauga. I was an only child, and not having our large extended family around us was isolating.

My mom, who was twenty-six when we arrived, was homesick. She began wearing a hijab. My dad insisted she take it off because he didn't want people to think we were terrorists. They argued for months but he wore her down and she gave in.

My mom and I are light, olive-skinned, but my dad is

darker and at that time he had a serious moustache. It was as black and bushy as they came. A visibly Arab man with that kind of facial hair would arguably get the same reaction, or worse, as a woman wearing a hijab. Moustaches were trendy at the time but still, if he was so concerned about appearances, you'd think he would have looked in the mirror. He saw Tom Selleck; racists saw Saddam Hussein.

My parents only spoke English with me at home because they feared I wouldn't learn the language properly and would be ostracized. Thinking about this makes my chest ache, because I wish more than anything that I was fluent in Arabic. They meant well.

On the other hand, my mom nagged me to pray for years. My family would say *Bismillah al rahman al rahim* (the beginning of a sura and the first verse in the Qur'an) before eating, before starting the car, before doing most things really. I'd only say it if I was scared, worried, or suffering. Like the time I went on the SlingShot at Canada's Wonderland with my best friend.

The two of us were strapped into a harness and hoisted about three hundred feet in the air. Before being catapulted down, one of us was supposed to pull a lever. As my friend did the honours, I recited a sura out loud. She'd never heard me do this in her life, so I'm pretty sure she thought we were going to die. We survived and proceeded to go on the ride two more times.

*

Then there was the ritual of my mom sending me to Egypt during summer breaks so that I could maintain a connection to my family and culture. There were a few summers in my pre-teens when I would have preferred hanging out with my friends in Scarborough. But looking back, I'm glad she insisted I go. I spent time with my family in the way I always wished we could in Canada, day-to-day, sharing all the big and small life moments.

As for Christmas, I lived vicariously through not only cartoons but also the sitcom TV specials of my favourite shows—big families coming together and loving each other despite their endearing flaws. *Full House, Family Matters, Home Improvement, The Fresh Prince of Bel-Air.* They never mentioned religion; I suppose to appeal to a wider audience. And it worked. When it was just my mom and me, Christmas felt safe, comfortable and a little magical.

A couple of years after the divorce, my mom fell in love with a Catholic man, Mike—a big deal for her. In Egypt, there's a law that states that a Muslim woman cannot marry a non-Muslim man. A Muslim man, however, can marry a non-Muslim woman. She kept their relationship secret from our family in Egypt for a long time.

I was grateful that she met him, in a way, because I knew I would probably end up with someone who wasn't Muslim. One summer in Egypt, my grandparents introduced me to a young boy. I was around ten years old. My grandmother, aunt, and I had lunch with him and his family. To the naked eye, it was an innocent get-together. I discovered later, from my aunt who has no filter with me, that it was an early introduction to see if we would be a good match for marriage one day. Nothing ever came of it, and it wasn't brought up again, but that was when I started to think about the idea of marriage and how it worked. I understood that a Muslim man seeks out a certain type of woman, and his family in particular wants their son to marry a "good Muslim woman." I knew, even as a kid, that would never be me. I already questioned a lot of my religion and didn't abide by most of the rules. As a teen and twenty-something, forget about it—I was pretty much the poster child of what a "good Muslim woman" shouldn't be. Not eating pork was the only rule I ever stayed consistent with and even with that one I faltered.

In Grade 6, I ate bacon-flavoured chips by accident. After the second chip I took the bag from my friend who'd offered them, to see what flavour they were. The word 'Bacon' was written in fun bold letters. I froze. My eternity flashed before my eyes. Fireballs, dragon heads, a goateed Satan on a throne cackling while I writhed in pain. I ate another handful. My fate was sealed after that first chip; I figured I might as well go all out if, either way, I was going to hell. My tastebuds rejoiced, my stomach demanded more,

*

and my friend saved me from myself by snatching the bag back, dumping the last crumbs into her mouth. It was only later in life that I realized bacon flavouring doesn't contain any actual pork.

As far as I could tell, my mom followed everything by the book religion-wise, until she made an exception for Mike. He was nice but so awkward.

I would find him sleeping on our couch Saturday mornings when I woke up to watch cartoons. He made an effort with me but our conversations were filled with awkward pauses and too much eye contact. Sometimes we would sit in silence and then, just as I was leaving a room, he would start an animated discussion. I did my best to humour him but I would ultimately have to abandon him mid-sentence and moonwalk out.

Their relationship became serious. They bought a house in Richmond Hill. It was massive compared to the modest apartment we left behind. The Hill was about forty-five minutes away, but I might as well have moved countries. Back then, there were fewer strip malls and more farmland. It was quieter with less traffic and felt pretty white. Total culture shock.

I missed Scarborough and all my friends deeply. Plus the timing was colossal. I was starting high school and knew no one. I wish I could say that I was a sexy-grunge-type outcast or a manic pixie dream girl—the quirky chick with colourful hair whose whimsical nature inspires boys to appreciate a new outlook on life. The closest I ever came was when I bleached my hair to get it so red that you could spot me from miles away.

But alas, I was the weird girl who made jokes nobody found funny and who wouldn't take off her jacket. It was a purplish-blue nylon coat. There was nothing special about it, but I never wanted to take that thing off. Sometimes my teachers would prompt me, but I was stubborn. I'd say, "No, I'm good." I really wasn't.

Many of the school's students were Jewish and didn't celebrate Christmas, not even in a secular way. The holiday excitement focused more on the two weeks off.

One time, when everyone flooded outside and idled in groups speaking loudly and laughing, a girl intercepted me. I had my eyes down and was heading to the bus stop. Her gaggle of minions inched within earshot. The girl wore a shit-eating grin. "Maybe Santa will bring you a new jacket this year."

Her friends laughed.

My face flushed. "Yeah, maybe." I shrugged and walked away, nonchalant. I wanted to die.

In Richmond Hill, Christmas had become something else. It was lonely. We exchanged gifts. Mike went to midday Mass alone. We had turkey. I'd sneak outside to smoke a joint, then scurry up to my room to listen to Pink Floyd's *The Wall* on my headphones. I'd lie in bed staring at the ceiling, transported. The melancholy tone and quiet rage resonated with me. It was my escape from everyone and became my private world to go to. I was beginning to let go of the idea of magic. It was just another holiday.

What really killed it was the time my mom forced me to go to Mike's parents' house. I wanted to stay home alone.

"On Christmas?" Her voice rose an octave.

"Why do you care so much, anyway? You're not even Christian."

She rolled her eyes and told me to get dressed. I stormed into my room, slammed my door, and threw on baggy jeans and a hockey hoodie. She looked me up and down at the front door with disdain. I pretended not to notice.

They were nice enough, but being around them made me feel like an interloper. They forced themselves to be polite with empty small talk and strained smiles. I sat in the living room alone while everyone was in the kitchen and, to pass the time, ate a box of After Eight chocolates I found on the side table. My step-grandmother walked in and looked at the wrappers. She snatched the box. Our eyes locked. "Did you finish these?"

"Umm, yeah, I guess?"

"You finished ALL of them?" She waved the box in my face.

I stared at her and took the box. "Sorry."

She yelled at me to put the box and wrappers in the garbage and followed me to make sure that I did.

My mom must have heard something and came out of the kitchen, but I waved her away as if to say it's fine.

I was shaking but kept my composure. For the rest of the evening, I remained silent.

That was a long time ago. Over the years, we managed to co-exist at family events, even funerals. I became close for a time with one of Mike's sisters and niece. They were less uptight and they shared the dry humour that was more in my wheelhouse. His dad was also very kind. So, I did find my place but I never felt comfortable. I buried my feelings and tried to make the best of it and kept moving forward.

I met Eoghan (Owen) after I graduated from York University and was living alone in the Beaches. He was Irish and in Canada on a work visa. Our relationship was a whirlwind. Partying, going to concerts. We drove to Lollapalooza in Chicago after one month of dating. Ten hours in a car with a new boyfriend. Risky, but it paid off. I discovered we never ran out of things to talk about, and he just got me. Other guys I'd dated would offer a sympathy chuckle at my weird jokes, but he not only belly laughed, he would take the joke even further.

I met his parents a few months into our relationship

when they flew to Toronto to visit. We took them to the CN Tower restaurant, and I couldn't eat my hundred-dollar dinner and picked at my cuticles until they bled. We talked about the city and Canadian culture. I asked them about Eoghan's band, The Kringe, that he was in before he moved to Canada.

"Cringeworthy," they said.

"Punk rock isn't really their scene," Eoghan said.

They told me how they once went to see him play and saw him roar into a mic, guzzle a mickey of vodka, then jump around the stage in skinny jeans, topless.

I was in love.

That November, Eoghan became gloomy. He would be missing Christmas in Ireland for the first time in his life. His dad had told him he'd be better off saving his money and not to put any pressure on himself to make it back.

He asked what we would do for Christmas over here. I shrugged and said, "Dinner at my mom's, I guess."

His eyes shifted. "So, just like Thanksgiving?"

"I dunno. There'll be a tree."

His face went blank and his eyes widened. He couldn't get over the fact that it would be just the four of us like any other dinner at their place. I poured two generous glasses of wine then asked him to tell me what Ireland was like at that time of year.

He told me about his family and all the interesting

complex characters within it. Friends he'd known since childhood who he missed but hadn't spoken to much since he'd been away because he wasn't a phone person. He talked about everyone coming together in the village of Ballyduff where he was raised—family, friends, acquaintances—sharing the same space and joy. About Irish trad music and sing-a-longs. Lock-ins—when the pub was officially closed, but unofficially the party raged on behind closed blinds and a bolted door.

"You kind of have to be there to really get it," he said.

"It sounds amazing."

"Fuck it. Will we go back?"

"We?" My eyes bulged.

"Yeah. Christmas in Ireland and you can meet everyone."

I'd never been to Europe and missing Christmas with my mom and stepdad was no big deal. This was exciting. But as the departure date drew closer, I started to panic.

Was I really doing this? Would his sisters be bitches? Nobody ever worries about the boyfriend's brother. But what if he didn't like me?

One of my friends suggested baking cookies and bringing them in a tin for them. I had never baked a thing in my life. I shared this brilliant idea with Eoghan. He was horrified— as if I'd told him I was planning to hand out condoms or T-shirts with my face on them.

"They will take the piss out of you relentlessly for that.

It's not you. Don't do things that aren't you. They don't give a shit if you bake cookies."

We flew from Toronto to London, then London to Cork. Eoghan's dad picked us up from the airport, and it was a forty-five-minute drive to Ballyduff, population five hundred. It was pitch black, and the roads became progressively bumpier.

I noted, "There's no streetlights. It's so dark."

His dad turned the high beams on to humour me, and I instantly regretted opening my tourist mouth.

It was Christmas Eve, and everyone was going to Mass. The only place I wanted to go was to bed, but it was easier to pretend it was no big deal and do my best to blend in.

The church was small and made of stone. It was crowded, but people knew each other. Everyone was excited to see Eoghan and no doubt a little curious about the girl he brought home from Canada. Many waved or turned in their seats and nodded hello. One of his cousins sat in front of us and asked me what I thought of the church.

"It's cozy," I said.

"Cozy." He laughed.

I internally groaned and hoped I wouldn't say any more dumb shit.

Everyone bent and kneeled in unison and repeated words that were foreign to me. I bit my lip and shifted in my seat.

If I don't bend and kneel, is it rude? If I do, am I betraying something about myself?

Nobody was paying attention to me, but I felt like I stood out because I was the only person there who was not Catholic. When it was finally near the end, a choir sang from the gallery above. Everyone around me stood and started shaking hands. They offered peace. My heart raced. My face grew tomato-red. I was in a church in rural Ireland, which I had yet to see in daylight. I was jet-lagged, trying to be normal, doing my best to make a good impression.

For the longest time, I told myself I didn't care about being accepted, about my fractured family, being "cool,'" churches, whatever. Christmas with Pink Floyd was all I needed. If I didn't care, I avoided the pain, but I didn't realize until much later that I was also avoiding the joy. It didn't matter then. But it did now.

I mumbled, "Peace be with you."

When I stepped out into the cold, I was happy it was done. I watched my breath form clouds in the air and realized I was just happy.

There were four pubs in the village. One was off limits because it was mainly frequented by the older men in the area. We did a pub crawl of the other three. Eoghan's parents, siblings, aunts, uncles, and cousins spread out to them. Eoghan and I went to The Log Cabin. There he spoke with dozens of people. Big smiles and handshakes. I felt like I was with the mayor. They told me I was with a great guy. I heard several versions of the same story about Eoghan performing a show with his band where he fell off the stage onto a group of children.

I bought the next round of drinks. Eoghan asked for a pint of Guinness. The bartender poured the pint halfway and disappeared. Hello? Did she forget about me or what? I nearly took the drink.

A woman grabbed my elbow. "They haven't finished the pour!"

"Huh?"

"They pour three quarters and wait for it to turn black before pouring the rest."

I pressed a palm to my heart and thanked her before placing the glass back on the bar. She winked and nodded. I remain grateful to her. I'm pretty sure I would have never lived it down if I had brought the half-poured pint back.

I was surrounded by a tight-knit community where everyone knew each other. Even so, when I drifted to the periphery, someone would come over to talk with me. It was a great night and I got hammered.

To say we were hungover the next day would be an understatement. I'm not a puker, but I had a pounding headache and was gasping for water. I ate something small for breakfast with Eoghan's nana. She told us to get ready because Eoghan's dad would pick us up for Christmas dinner soon. Dinner? I glanced at the clock. It was noon.

I whispered to Eoghan, "When's dinner?"

"I think one."

I scrunched my face. Dinner for lunch it is.

Eoghan's family home was only a couple of minutes away. We could have walked but it was especially cold with the strong winds that day. I gawked out the window of the car, my first chance to see Ballyduff in daylight. The house sat atop a hill overlooking the Blackwater River, hedgerows, and bright green fields for miles. Cows on patches of grass if I squinted. It was breathtaking.

"You coming in?" Eoghan asked.

I stood at the edge of the driveway, staring down, my hair blowing around me. It was like looking at a painting. "Holy shit. This view is amazing."

After dinner I had a few hours to rest before Eoghan's extended family would be there. Around 7:00 pm, one of his aunts arrived and it wasn't long before the house was packed. It was hot and full of life and laughter. As the night progressed, the older group got into an intense game of cards, a game called Forty-Five, and Eoghan's nana was the one to beat. They chided each other and drank into the night. People dropped off one by one until it was just us and his siblings, bleary-eyed and talking in the living room. We fell asleep by the fire, while *Die Hard* played on the television.

The next morning, we woke up on different couches. We rubbed our heads and groaned. There was no time to nurse our hangovers. We were only in Ireland until the 28th and, for Stephen's Night, we were meeting some of Eoghan's friends in Cork.

The city had colourful old buildings by the harbour, large pedestrian areas and plenty of pubs and restaurants within walking distance. Eoghan and his friends were excited to show me their old haunts, and we went to the Crane Lane and Fred Zeppelin's. We drank, we danced.

We stumbled out of the club, searching for a place to eat. I was wearing heels and my feet hurt, so Eoghan gallantly offered to give me a piggy-back ride. My first instinct was to say "no way" because I was chubby and feared he would struggle to carry me. He was over six feet tall and in decent shape, so I swallowed my insecurities and embraced the manic pixie dream girl within. He hoisted me onto his back, and I "whooped" because I was very drunk.

He took exactly four steps before we went flying. He tripped and smashed his face into the ground, and I went sailing over him and landed on my chin. I stood up and pretended I was totally fine—nothing to see here.

We made it back to his friend's apartment and thankfully there was one sober person there who was not out with us.

He took one look at me and said, "Umm, you need to see a doctor."

It was the last thing I wanted to do. My head was spinning, and I needed to lie down. But sober guy insisted. It was bad. So we went to an urgent care, and I got six stitches in my chin. Eoghan needed a couple at the top of his nose between his eyes.

We slept at his friend's apartment in Cork and the next morning, Eoghan drove his dad's car back to Ballyduff. His aunt and her husband were hosting a big dinner for a large group of us. The closer we got to Ballyduff, the more nauseated I felt. I wasn't used to the winding, bumpy roads. They were so narrow too. Every time a car passed us, I closed my eyes. Tree branches scraped and rattled the side of the car. At one point, we stopped because there was a sheep in the middle of the road. I giggled and took a photo.

We laughed about the piggy-back ride gone wrong. He says that I cried when I fell and wailed, "My beautiful face," when the doctor said that I needed the stitches. I told him to shut up and that there's no way I said "beautiful."

At the dinner table, Eoghan's parents and siblings, his aunt and uncle who were hosting, another uncle and his wife who live up the road, and his lovely nana surrounded us. Eighty percent of us were hungover and quiet and everyone was asking us what the hell happened to our faces. What could we say but the truth?

I winced bracing myself for scolding or judgement—a lecture at the very least.

*

Eoghan's mom shook her head with a giant smile and said, "Ye are two of a kind."

I caught Eoghan's eye, and he winked. My stomach fluttered. His aunt insisted on taking family photos of all of us, and so we posed with bandaged faces and goofy grins. We left Ireland exhausted, but full of joy and relief that it had gone well, minus a few scrapes and bruises.

That first Christmas in Ireland will always hold a special place in my heart because it was the first time as an adult that I felt the magic, and it had nothing to do with gifts.

The Hitchhiker

ROB WOLF

I spent Christmas Eve away from my children and instead found myself with my in-laws-to-be, who hosted a block party for their friends every year. In retrospect, I might have been looking for a way to attach myself to this new family, and perhaps a bit too earnestly.

These people were kind and accepting, and I tried hard to fit in with them. They came from a different world. They had designer clothes, better décor, and fewer concerns about day to day survival.

I had hoped to convince myself that the life I was about to embark upon was really going to be okay, that these could be my people and I could feel safe among them. But less than an hour and one drink in, dread, the voice and constant companion of my anxiety, pulled me back to all the reasons I should feel awful about my decision to leave my first marriage and to enter another one.

I tried to make meaningful conversation with my hosts and a number of the guests about economics and psychology, my preferred subjects. I quickly realized that they preferred small talk and complaints about random things to substantial discourse. I asked a friend of my in-laws-to-be, a woman with heavy rings dripping from her fingers, if she thought all of the capitalistic splendour and consumption of the holiday season was just a way for all of us to assuage the collective guilt we felt about the inequality in the world.

She blinked slowly, took a long sip of her eggnog, and said, "I like Christmas. It reminds me that I'm not poor. I was poor once, you know. It wasn't all that great."

She turned on her heel and my face reddened. I guess I was having trouble reading the room.

Laura busied herself floating through the house offering drinks and smiles to all her parents' friends and neighbours. She read my inner turmoil and pulled me into the coat room, kissed me, and took my face in her hands.

"Darling, lighten up. It's Christmas. Everything is fine."

"I'm glad you think so. Maybe it's not. Maybe they're just filling a void, spending on so much . . . stuff, so they don't have to think about what it all means, how others are suffering while they indulge."

She looked bemused and a little sad. "Well, sulk if you like, it's up to you. I'm going to enjoy myself. I don't want to ruin our first Christmas."

I felt abandoned in that moment, as I later learned as a therapist, my inner child often did. I did something uncharacteristic. I let the urge to drink take over and downed too many stiff rum and eggnogs. The buzz settled in comfortably and took the edge off my simmering angst.

I'm not much of a drinker, but I was hoping it would make me less critical. It didn't.

I couldn't help thinking how inane their conversations were. About the price of gas, that the world economy was in the shitter, and that the Maple Leafs were two years away from being two years away. You know, the important stuff. Were they running from reality? But then again, wasn't I too? They commiserated with each other about the problems outside themselves, and I struggled alone on the inside with the meaning and consequence of the choices I had recently made, leaving my wife and family for Laura.

At one point, I walked up behind Laura and reached around to hug her and feel her warmth melt my sadness. Maybe even cop a feel and lure her into an empty room. I ended up lurching into her, almost knocking her off her feet. She turned and looked at me with fiery eyes. She hissed, "You're drunk, get yourself together, and don't embarrass me in front of everyone."

A few guests overheard and quickly averted their eyes. Red heat surged in my face, and I turned to leave the room, fumbling towards an exit. I crawled up the stairs on all fours and found the back spare bedroom and fell asleep in my clothes. It may have been the lowest I felt in my life.

3:30 am, Christmas day, my phone alarm jolted me from my abbreviated sleep. I got dressed, a bit too formally, in khakis and a button-down collar. I had a long day ahead, driving back to my old home in time to open gifts and then back to Laura's for Christmas dinner. The room was unfamiliar and I stumbled about, trying not to wake Laura. I whispered, "Merry Christmas."

She mumbled something softly and I closed the door.

Breakfast in the dark was coffee and a bellyful of the previous night's sweets that floated heavily on too many stiff eggnogs. A lot was dancing in my head, and my belly, but it sure as hell wasn't sugarplums.

I slid behind the wheel of my aging Subaru and aimed it east to the country, to make the three-hour drive back to the homeland, to my perplexed adolescent children and a freshly minted ex-wife, and my old family home, a place that had become for me, in its final years, a place of confinement.

I couldn't blame my ex-wife, Lisa, for why I needed a change. I had been locked inside our sheltered, rural community that was rife with religious compliance and repression, part of her family tradition. The twenty or so years I spent there led to a loss of my identity. I had gone along to get along for years, accepting the intellectual confines of her family's religion so that I could be part of something larger than my own directionless upbringing. It eventually beat me down emotionally until I was a shell of the man I wanted to be. It eventually came to a head and I had to make a choice: comply and stay part of the community or leave and be exiled, or so it felt. So, I did the only thing I could do to be honest with myself. I left to find a new road and hoped a new dawn might bring with it a return to the man, and the spark, I had lost along the way.

Yet here I was on the old road. Snow had come early that year and the talk of a white Christmas was on everyone's lips. Two big Nor' Easters had rolled up the east coast in the days before, bringing an easy wind and downy flakes. They left behind massive snow drifts, some as big as houses. They simultaneously brought a peaceful and cheery holiday feeling all the while making the month busier than usual and planning for the break more hectic as conditions delayed everyone's preparations and gift shopping.

Then a warm wind had descended from the heavens and the Maritime dampness multiplied its chilling effect. It was only plus two degrees, and it was bone-numbing as I pulled out of the driveway and onto the Trans-Canada in the pred-awn darkness. The road was barely visible. The combination of oncoming headlights and fog stabbed at my eyes. Luckily there weren't many other cars on the road. But the pre-dawn light revealed there would be no white Christmas. Driving rain and rising temperatures from the day before had shrunk the wind-sculpted drifts into huge, rounded mounds of grey sludge. The once lovely peaks of snow no longer disguised debris on the streets and roads and the highway was dark and lonely. I drove into what felt like the past.

*

The fog of war? Or the fog of self-deception?

I ruminated on how I wound up on this path. Nothing creeps as eerily through a misty darkness as self-doubt. I wanted to feel noble or even heroic as I deftly navigated my car around semi-frozen puddles and mentally scurried around self-condemnation. I did try to tell myself that I was a good guy here, and that I had made it through to the other side of a captivity in my first marriage. I couldn't stay and I felt like I had been upfront with my wife and myself, yet leaving also felt like I had ruptured a childhood longing to be part of something permanent. Me and my fucking perpetual abandonment issues. I convinced myself that the honesty I was searching for within my life would make me a better dad and person. I wanted to find some meaning in all of this heartache. This new life had yet to deliver any.

And then there were my children: Karey, Andy, and Austin. They had always been the three best reasons I had for getting up every day. Their love and belief in me allowed me to hope that I could persevere and someday know and embrace the value they already saw in me. Since their dad's upending of the family, I had done my best to nurture our relationship and allow them time to adapt. I was willing to do anything I could, including returning to them today, full of trepidation and doubt, to help them through the transition until we were able to thrive in our next chapters. I guess I hoped that I could ease my pain through validating them. It wasn't the perfect plan, but it was the best I could come up with. I wasn't sure how this visit would go, but as always, I was willing to put myself out there for them. If my journey today was to have any success, then just maybe we could find a sparkle of Christmas magic, like our little family had for so many years on these mornings. I sang and I wept as I pushed through the darkness and I hoped that this new, first Christmas would be the beginning of something better, something magic.

I thought music might help. And briefly it did—I sang along with Rose Cousins, *A New Kind of Light,* and one seasonal chestnut after another until the accumulation of memories turned me back down the road that I was now heading. All of these songs just reminded me of, and made me long for, happier days. It was hard to get my thoughts out from under the weight of the past and focus on the uncomfortable present. It wasn't working. I questioned my motives, my behaviour, and every decision I'd made in the past year yet again, but for the life of me couldn't figure out how I could do, or could have done, a damn thing differently.

Suddenly, my headlights found a pair of eyes in the fog, and a soggy creature emerged from the pre-dawn gloom. A hand stabbed towards me with a raised thumb in the darkness that sent a jolt through me. A quick scan revealed a man in a Cabela's hoodie, camo down vest, heavy rubber boots, and a ball cap.

At first glance, I thought it might be a walk of shame for some country kid, sneaking away from last night's hookup. I usually pick up hitchhikers, as I'd received lots of rides in my younger and poorer nomadic days. I'd had a few scary encounters on the road, both driving and getting driven, and time has made me less heedless. But I noticed he was carrying a brightly colored gift bag that didn't look worn or used. I went back and forth in my head debating whether I should let a stranger into my emotional turmoil. It might be a distraction, I thought, so a kilometre later I u-turned to find the lost soul.

He climbed in and stuck out a cold, wet hand in greeting.

"Merry Christmas. Thanks a lot for stopping. I'm Brent," said a boy's voice in a man's body. In the dome light, I saw the beginnings of what might someday grow into a beard on his chin and upper lip. His smile revealed tobacco stains and a strange delight. His energy and warmth didn't fit with the chilly morning scene we were a part of.

I replied, "I'm Rob, Merry Christmas to you too. Where are you heading?"

"Goin' to Aspen, but I'll go as far as you'll take me," he smiled. "I'm goin' to see my son. It's his, I mean our, first Christmas."

His joy was palpable—a first-time new dad.

Memories again hurled me backwards over a couple

of decades. Carols, cinnamon cider, magnificent feasts, sparkling ornaments, visions of assembling toys late on the nights before and screams of delight in the morning rushed into my head and welled up in my chest. A montage played itself out in my head, so many sweet memories filled with food and laughter pulled painfully into the present. The loss grabbed at my throat and I could barely speak. Guilt is a terrible thing to receive for Christmas.

He must have felt my retreat from the moment and rattled nervously on to fill in the silence.

"Yea, my son's mom and I aren't together no more, but she said I could come this morning to be with him. Well, after the lawyers got involved, she did. She allowed me coming to visit today, between seven and twelve, you know, but I figure she did that only 'cause she didn't think I'd show, I don't have no wheels yet, my truck broke down last week and I wanted to bring my boy a gift, so I didn't spend the money to get the truck fixed. I had to work last night at Tim's till ten when they closed and the bus isn't running today so I figured I'd at least try to hitch a ride. I really appreciate you stopping. My ex and me don't speak to each other that much, it always ends with a fight, but at least I'm allowed to see my boy today. His name is Jacob, Jake the Snake I calls him, haha! I'm not sure what's gonna happen when I get there, how it's gonna go, but I figured bein' there is all what matters . . ."

*

He hit a full head of steam as he railed on about his and his son's mother's torrid tales of shared misery and injustices. All the while I was glad to let him go on, as I gathered myself, trying to sort the memories, heartaches and self-condemnation this moment was bringing back. I'm not sure when I lost contact with his voice.

" 'Scuse me . . .I said, how far are you going?"

"Sorry," I replied, "You reminded me of something. Um . . . I'm heading to Eden Lake, but it's not very far, I'll take you to Aspen, no problem."

"Geez, that's real good of you, alright!"

As daylight began to seep into the mist, we rambled on, sharing stories as men have a way of doing, talking about something seemingly unimportant but thinking about, and meaning, something else that isn't.

"I wanted to give Jake something he'd remember me from, 'cause I don't get to see him every day. So, I got him a monster truck with King Cobra on it." He pointed toward the brightly coloured and slightly soggy gift bag, "I'm studying heavy duty mechanics at NSCC. My dad ran equipment before he died and it's all I've ever really wanted to do. Of course, I got Jake some camo too," Brent said with a chuckle as he pulled out a small child's ball cap.

I talked about being a father. I told him of my sons, about their sports and their aspirations. I talked on about the things I got to teach them to do, and the confidence I hoped they'd get from it. I told him my daughter was beautiful, sensitive, a little quirky, sang like a bird, and had the gift to fill up a room with joy.

"I'll bet they're all just like the old man," Brent smiled.

"Maybe. I hope so," I replied too quickly. His compliment surprised me.

I told him where I was going and the situation I faced. I guess I felt it was okay to unload a few things as I'd likely never see him again, and he was, after all, captive in my car. He listened more than I expected. I was careful not to preach about fatherhood too much, as I am prone to do. With me looking at fatherhood in the rearview, as it were, and him looking ahead, it didn't seem fair for me to be over-bearing about it.

As we rolled down the hill to his journey's end, he grew quiet and I understood. We never know how a moment like this will turn out. We never quite know how our gestures of love and the vulnerability that goes with them will be received. The exuberance we build on road trips often has a way of dissipating when our destination and the stark reality of our situation emerge. Our best intentions often get mis-interpreted by others.

"Well, here goes nothing," he sighed as we slowed to the driveway.

"Listen," I said, "no matter what happens with his mom, for all of your lives, you and Jake, but mostly you, will always know how important being here is today. You know showing up is sometimes the only thing we can do, and we have to trust the process that it will be enough."

"Thanks, man," said Brent. "Being here is so worth it."

"Merry Christmas, Brent. Give Jake a high five for me."

"Merry Christmas, Rob. Thanks for the ride and the talk," he said as he and his gift slipped out.

He beamed a bright smile under his ball cap as he closed the door. "This is what it's all about, man."

He turned, shoulders high, and made toward a small country house stirring with the first lights of the new day.

As I turned around and aimed my car back up the hill to Eden Lake, I allowed myself an uncustomary twinkling of satisfaction and pride. I'm not perfect, I'm not great at much, but I knew in that moment that I was the man I wanted to be and knew that it would matter.

I saw my old home rise out of the fog before me. I pulled into the familiar driveway and cut the engine and for a few minutes I drank in the silence. One by one the windows began to glow, and the house came to life with the magic and memories of old Christmases past. I didn't feel dread and remorse, only gratitude. I stood outside the door and heard Karey's voice, brimming with excitement, calling on her brothers to get up and get dressed.

"Dad is here, Dad is here!"

She had, of course, been up watching and waiting

for who knows how long for my headlights to pierce the darkness. The magic and excitement in those words, spoken every Christmas morning for many years by her or one of her brothers, were why I made the trek. I breathed a deep sigh and in a moment of quiet exhilaration, I knew that I had made the right decision.

Contributors

Lareina Abbott pens Métis-themed speculative fiction and memoir with a tie to the spiritual and natural world, and to ancestry. She received the Writers Guild of Alberta 2023 Howard O'Hagan award for her story "Ma Soeur Marie," and is an Audible Indigenous Writers Circle alumni. She currently writes in Calgary/Mohkinstsis. @boneblackstories.

Lillian Au is a former spokesperson and TV journalist. She works in radio as a traffic anchor. She received an honourable mention for one of her stories for the International Amy MacRae Award for Memoir. Lillian lives with her husband and two children on Vancouver's North Shore.

Sarah El Sioufi is an Egyptian Canadian whose unpublished manuscript won the Muskoka Novel Marathon and was longlisted for the Santa Fe Writers Project Literary Award. Her work has also appeared in *Queen's Quarterly.* She lives in Algonquin Highlands, Ontario, with her husband and two children.

Averill Groeneveld-Meijer grew up in The Hague before moving to Vancouver. She has a BA and MA in Historical Geography from UBC and a certificate in creative writing. She has been published in the *Maine Review,* shortlisted for the place-writing issue of *Hinterland* magazine, and is currently completing a memoir of her experiences growing up in the Netherlands as a Canadian.

Jane Harris is a Canadian poet, essayist, and author. She was awarded an Alberta Literary Award for Short Non-fiction and placed third in the Susan Crean Surrey Muse non-fiction competition. Jane is the author of two creative non-fiction books and her essays appear in anthologies published by University of Alberta Press.

Jill Maynard has deep connections in her communities of Deep Cove and Saltspring Island. She writes about her experiences as a mom of three, a teacher of at-risk youth as well as her explorations in nature. A student of creative writing, this is her first formal publication.

Michael McLean holds an undergraduate degree in Criminology and spent a lifetime serving the community as a law enforcement professional. It is his firm belief that silence is a stagnant pool in the wellspring of our convictions. But when we taste these waters, we begin to speak truth, and carve channels of change through the landscape of our apathy.

Jennifer Pownall has had her writing published in *The New York Times, The Globe and Mail*, and several anthologies. She lives in Port Coquitlam where she serves as the arts council's Director of Literary Arts and recently had a piece installed on the Donald Storywalk. Jennifer is passionate about checking items off her ever-expanding bucket list.

Jolène Savoie-Day holds a degree in Journalism and a Master's in Leadership. She is a school board trustee, a marathoner, and a triathlete. She plays French horn in a community orchestra and has a collection of colourful ukuleles. She lives in Ottawa with her husband, two kids, and their bow-wearing dog. Jolène is currently working on her first memoir chronicling her mental health journey with both humour and heart.

Elizabeth Somboun is the award-winning author of the autobiography, *Elevators of My Life,* and is a published poet. She has a degree in social work and, when not writing, helps people overcome the impossible. She lives in a quaint Ontario village that has epic scope for the imagination.

Léa Taranto is a disabled Chinese Jewish Canadian writer who lives with OCD and comorbid disorders. An MFA graduate of the University of British Columbia, her debut novel, *A Drop in the Ocean*, will be published in May 2025. She resides on traditional, unceded Halkomelem and Squamish territories in BC.

Rob Wolf is a writer and performer of songs, musicals and plays living in Guysborough County, Nova Scotia. A therapist by day, he likes to write about rural people, exploring complex and diverse characters. His stories have been published online and in print. He recently self-published his first novel, *Ashanti.*

Enjoyed these Christmas epiphanies?
Read more true-life stories in . . .

BETTER

NEXT

YEAR

EDITED BY JJ LEE

Available from booksellers everywhere or from the
publisher, tidewaterpress.ca